D1355894

Toolbox Guides for Security Technicians

Edited by John Sanger

Basic Alarm Electronics
John Sanger

Electronic Locking Devices
John L. Schum

Upcoming Volumes

Intrusion Detection Devices: Perimeter Protection
John Sanger

Intrusion Detection Devices: Interior Protection
John Sanger

Other Guides in Preparation

Intrusion Alarm Control Equipment
Intrusion Alarm Signalling Equipment
Alarm System Power Supplies and Batteries
Peripheral Alarm System Devices
Alarm Installing Tools and Equipment
Specialized Emergency Protection Systems

Electronic Locking Devices

JOHN L. SCHUM

Butterworths
Boston   London   Singapore   Sydney   Toronto   Wellington

Library of Congress Cataloging-in-Publication Data

Schum, John L.
    Electronic locking devices.

    Bibliography: p.
    Includes index.
    1. Electronic locking devices.   I. Title.
TH9735.S38 1988   683'.3   87-21865
ISBN 0-409-90125-3

British Library Cataloguing in Publication Data

Schum, John L.
    Electronic locking devices.
    1. Electronic locking devices   2. Door fittings
    I. Title
    683'.32   TH9735

    ISBN 0-409-90125-3

Butterworth Publishers
80 Montvale Avenue
Stoneham, MA 02180

10 9 8 7 6 5 4 3 2 1

Printed in the United States of America

Contents

About the Series

The job of protection is a serious one. Every year in the United States, more home and business owners find peace of mind through the installation of security systems. They depend on their alarm systems to function properly—their lives and property are at stake. To assist security professionals in fulfilling their obligation to customers, this series—Toolbox Guides for Security Technicians—has been created.

These volumes compile information on every aspect of alarm system planning, design, installation, service, and troubleshooting—information that will complement existing skills or become the foundation of a fledgling career. Whether you are looking for the solution to a design problem or installation snag, or seeking tips on running wire or foiling windows, this series will serve you. It is a reference library on security—the first of its kind.

Each volume is devoted to a specific topic, starting with basic alarm electronics and electronic locking devices. Subsequent works will discuss different equipment types and applications, including interior and perimeter protection devices, control panels, power supplies and batteries, signaling and monitoring systems, and outdoor protection systems. One book will be devoted to both little known and widely used tools for alarm installation and troubleshooting. Another will be dedicated to wireless intrusion detection systems. In every volume, the authors provide tips that uncomplicate difficult tasks or simply save a few minutes of installation time.

So comprehensive is this series that the authors recognized the need for one volume to serve as a reference work for the others. This companion guide will pull together the important material contained in the other texts. Here you will find conversion tables, resistance charts, color codes, and Ohm's law, along with an installer's dictionary of security terms. Instead of thumbing through hundreds of pages searching for one piece of data, you will be able to find the information quickly in this consolidated, easy-to-use volume.

Because reliability and accuracy are essential, the contributors to this series have solid alarm industry backgrounds. Some have experience in security equipment manufacturing; many are security dealers with years of installation or service experience; others, like myself, are journalists specializing in the security field. All the contributors and writers have been selected carefully for their expertise by John Sanger, an editor with the industry's leading security publication, *Security Distributing & Marketing,* and a former alarm company owner.

Mr. Sanger, coordinator of the series and coauthor of most books, will review each work to help ensure thoroughness in content and unity in style and presentation. The material in this series has been selected with you—the security professional—in mind. The facts in these books can work for you. Read them, understand them, apply them—and watch yourself grow.

Anne Lobel Armel

Preface

The intent of this book is to equip members of the hardware and security industry with the information they need to profit in the rapidly growing electronic security field. Its purpose is to educate and serve as a basic reference manual for those who desire increased knowledge of today's sophisticated electronic security equipment. A ground-floor opportunity exists today for a very profitable career in this widely accepted and fast-growing market. It is hoped that through the knowledge gained from this book, you will increase your participation in this field.

The contents of this book are meant to appeal to a wide range of professionals who are presently involved in the door hardware industry. Whether you install, purchase, design, or specify mechanical or electrical hardware, your present knowledge will be enhanced by this text. For locksmiths, hardware spec writers, architects, or security consultants, a knowledge of electric hardware and its use is a necessity in today's advanced door control and security systems.

It has become increasingly apparent that the lack of understanding of electronic products and their coordination within a door control system has caused confusion in all areas of this field. Personnel thoroughly qualified in mechanical hardware are reluctant to become involved with electronic hardware. Specifications are vague, and coordination of mechanical and electrical hardware is nonexistent or is being done by a very few individuals who are knowledgeable in both fields.

This book is a concerted effort to coordinate and explain the great volume of technical information put forth by electronic security product manufacturers. It is meant to be a simple guide and instruction manual, answering many of the questions that have arisen regarding the use of electronic hardware.

The text is written in language that the average person can understand. No attempt is made, nor is it necessary, to probe deeply into electronic theory. The text will provide a brief overview of basic electricity only to the extent needed to develop a proper electric locking system. It will provide extensive discussions of the various types of electric locking devices, access control and monitoring equipment, and low-voltage power supplies—their application, selection, and installation. Related equipment, simple systems, and troubleshooting techniques will also be covered.

In using this book, you should consider it a reference manual for the many components that may be necessary to resolve specific situations. By applying the knowledge you will gain, you will develop the skills necessary to piece together a complete system that is applicable to your particular problem. The information presented is organized in such a manner as to help you understand the procedures involved in solving variations of the example systems provided herein. It would be impossible in a book of this size to present the multitude of system variations you will be confronted with. This book will, however, supply you with all the components of the most widely used systems, which should be sufficient for your understanding and building of any system.

As you complete the first chapters of this book, devoted to the component parts of a system, you will gain confidence in your understanding of the basic systems presented in following chapters. A later chapter is devoted to basic troubleshooting, which, with a little practice, can save you many expensive hours in the field.

The contents of this text are based on current practices in the security field and actual problem areas that recur most often. The information gathered here has derived from extensive personal experience and many hours of scrutinizing manufacturers' technical literature. Once you have mastered your own methods, much of the information that is now available to you will be more useful than ever before.

This book is not necessarily complete, as actual situations may vary greatly. You should use professional consultants, manufacturers' engineering services, and the like, for specific or unusual applications.

J.L.S.

1

Why Electric Hardware?

Before answering the question asked in the title of this chapter, it may be best to review the history of locks. As you will see, access control was a concern from the very beginning of locking.

A BRIEF HISTORY OF LOCKING

A lock is a mechanical device for securing a door or receptacle so that it cannot be opened except by a key or by a series of manipulations that can be carried out only by a person knowing the secret or code.— *Encyclopaedia Britannica* (15th ed.), Vol. 11

It is difficult to say when the first lock was invented. Without doubt, the concept evolved as far back as the Neolithic Age, thousands of years ago. When people began to farm, and tended to live in one area, they certainly accumulated possessions that they could not carry about with them. Tools and harvest were too valuable to be left unguarded.

Perhaps the first solution to securing an opening was as simple as rolling a large stone in front of a cave entrance. But if the cave dweller could move a large stone, so could a thief! The trick would be to provide a hidden means of preventing the movement of the stone.

1

Only those who knew the secret would be able to enter. It is possible that a wedge buried beneath the stone, its location known only to a select few, became the world's first "key."

In 1842, what is believed to be the oldest lock in existence was discovered at Khorsabad, the ancient capital of Persia. Its design was attributed to Egypt. This Egyptian lock, which dates back possibly 4,000 years, is a pin-tumbler type.

Greek locks, which followed Egyptian locks, were more primitive in design, but the Greeks are credited with inventing the keyhole. The Romans introduced metal locks and invented the warded lock. In the Middle Ages, Spanish, German, and French artisans introduced a high degree of workmanship in lockmaking.

The locks used today were developed during the Industrial Revolution (see Figure 1–1). The following chronology outlines major events in lockmaking. (Some of the books listed in the Bibliography at the end of this book provide interesting stories relating to these developments.)

1778—The Barron lock: In England, Robert Barron patents a double-acting tumbler lock. This design remains the basis for all lever locks.

1784—The Bramah lock: In England, Joseph Bramah develops a lock that works on an entirely different principle. More secure than the Barron lock, it remains "unpickable" until 1851, when American locksmith A. C. Hobbs succeeds in picking it.

1818—The Chubb lock: Jeremiah Chubb of England improves upon the Barron lock. He incorporates a "detector" to defeat picking, which also shows whether a lock has been tampered with. In 1851, A. C. Hobbs succeeds in picking this lock, too.

1848—The Yale lock: American Linus Yale patents a pin-tumbler lock based on a variation of the ancient Egyptian lock.

1851—The Newell lock: Robert Newell exhibits his lock, made by Day and Newell of New York, at the Great Exhibition of 1851 in London. There is no record that it has ever been picked.

1860—The Yale lock: In the 1860s, Linus Yale, Jr., produces the Yale cylinder lock. It is probably the most familiar lock in the world today and is used universally for outside doors.

1873—The time lock: James Sargent of New York devises a lock that can be opened only at a preset time. This lock is based on an earlier Scottish patent.

Since the late 1800s, other locks have appeared with many specialized functions. Although numerous variations exist, the basic mechanical types in use today are Bramah, lever, Yale, and combination locks.

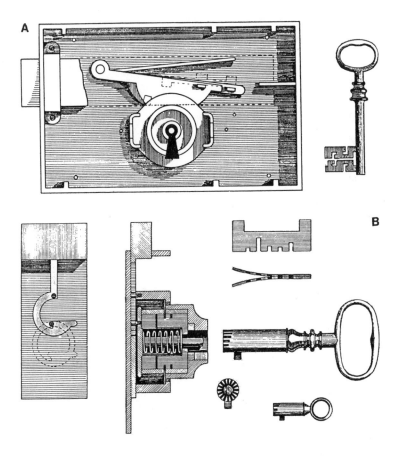

Figure 1–1.   Early locks. (A) The Barron lock, 1778. (B) The Bramah lock, 1784. (Courtesy of the Lock Museum of America, Terryville, CT)

I know of no written history of electric locks, other than my own research notes. What follows here is my attempt to put together all the bits and pieces of information that do exist. It should provide a fairly accurate record of the course of electric locking.

1886: Patent No. 353,263, dated November 23, 1886, was issued to Adam Lungen of New York for an electric door-opener.

1887–94: Eleven other patents for electric strikes were issued, all to inventors from New York and New Jersey.

1900: In the early 1900s, the Edwards Company, founded in 1872 by Robert Edwards, produced the forerunner of today's electric strike. These devices were used for apartments in New York's brownstone buildings. The original devices were powered by 6-volt batteries.

1910: A similar electric strike was produced around this time by the Francis Kyle Company of the Bronx, New York. Originally started in 1876, this large hardware company would later become the Trine Company.

1912: The Folger Adam Company, founded by Folger Adam, entered the market with an electric strike for special security applications. These strikes were originally handmade, relatively expensive devices.

1930: During the 1930s, the Francis Kyle Company became the Trine Company.

1951: Perhaps the first solenoid-operated bolt was developed by Dick Lockman, then employed by Schwabacher Hardware. Lockman later produced another version of the electric bolt at the Grigg Builders Supply Company.

1958–68: Throughout this decade, the solenoid-operated bolt line was further developed and refined by Dick Lockman and Bob Cerf, Jr., at the Challenger Lock Company. These devices were popular in electric bathroom interlocks, which until then were composed of mechanical locks or electric strikes wired in reverse. This line of electric locks was marketed under the trade name LOCK TRONIC. It was also during this time that Lockman and Cerf developed a magnetic door holder, which was displayed in the early 1960s at a trade show in Chicago (a predecessor of the later Doors and Hardware Institute trade shows). The door holder may have been an offshoot of the bulkhead door holder that had been used on ships for many years. It also would become the basis of the electromagnetic locking device.

1968: During the late 1960s, the need was recognized for a locking device for exit doors without a bolt that could cause a binding condition. At Challenger Lock Company, Lockman, Cerf, and Irv Saphirstein began toying with the idea of a lock made up of several magnetic door holders put together. The first electromagnetic locks were delivered by Challenger in October 1968 for the Forum in Montreal. In December 1968, Challenger Lock Company closed, and the LOCK TRONIC line of solenoid bolts was picked up and marketed by Eaton, Yale and Towne, Inc., of Rye, New York. The electromagnet was not included in the line.

1969–70: Sapherstein formed Locknetics, the company that pioneered the development of an electromagnetic locking device marketed under the trade name POWERLOCK.

1975: Another type of electric locking device was added when Von Duprin, Inc., electrified the door exit device.

1976–86: In the past ten years, many new manufacturers of electric locking devices have appeared and some older companies have expanded their product lines. The original companies that developed the aforementioned locking devices are all still in business, most with changes in ownership: Edwards, a unit of General Signal; Trine Security Products of Square D Company; Folger Adam Company; Yale Security Products Division of Scovill; Locknetics Security Products, a division of H. B. Ives; and Von Duprin, part of Ingersoll-Rand.

WHY ELECTRIC LOCKING DEVICES?

Having read the foregoing brief history of locking, you may already know some of the reasons electric locking devices evolved. Although mechanical locking systems have protected property and human life for centuries, they have always required extensive manpower to control, monitor, and maintain.

In a multidoor system, each opening must be manually locked and unlocked. If the system is in a public-access building, scheduled manual stops must be made at openings designated as free access/ egress during certain hours. Each locking device requires periodic maintenance because of wear and tear on mechanical moving parts, and periodic inspection is required to determine whether tampering has occurred. Control over the distribution of keys must be strictly enforced or the security of the system may be compromised. Resetting or replacing locks is a necessary nuisance when you don't know who has keys to a system or when those who hold keys are no longer to be allowed access to the system.

Another important problem arises when the security of a system interferes with personal safety. For example, chained panic devices on fire exit doors—an attempt to "improve" the security of the opening—have often led to the injury or death of innocent victims. Although this practice is far from legal, it is still being done.

Certainly, mechanical locking will continue to have a great many applications in our daily lives. However, in the not too distant past, our locking needs began to expand. Life-styles quickly became fast-paced and more complex. Giant buildings appeared, and institutions, hospitals, and schools became almost cities within themselves. Crime increased, and property worth thousands of dollars became property worth millions. Crimes against people also took on a new dimension.

As traditional crime increased, other crimes—such as industrial and political espionage and terrorism—began to become everyday events. Thus, not only has the need for crime prevention increased, but anxiety and fear have led to an unprecedented demand for security systems.

In the past ten to fifteen years, the security industry has grown by leaps and bounds. New products and systems have appeared to deal with ever-increasing problems. As we will see, the relatively new industry of electronic locking and monitoring devices offers many answers to our new problems and new security needs.

WHAT IS ELECTRIC SECURITY HARDWARE?

Electric hardware provides a versatile and flexible means of controlling an opening. Many different devices fall into the electric security hardware category, including locking devices, door holders, exit devices, automatic door operators, and alarm and monitoring equipment.

Although the electric lock is the main subject of this book, a brief discussion of the other devices will be provided in Chapter 3. As we will see later, all types of electric hardware can be coordinated success-fully with the electric lock. The electric lock—an easily controlled and monitored device—operates at safe, low voltages. It offers a means of security that does not compromise and in some ways complements life safety.

WHAT IS AN ELECTRIC LOCKING SYSTEM?

The concern of a security system is to employ certain products and systems to authorize, restrict, or deny ingress and egress of people and/ or vehicles into or within a building or area. The purpose of this control is to protect the property itself, its contents, or the people living or working within it.

A criminal—whether a company employee or a professional—can be shrewd, daring, and often treacherous. His biggest advantage is surprise; only he knows when he will strike. A security system must be designed to minimize the effects of an illegal incident. Each system must be custom designed to suit the specific need for which it is intended. Besides security and life safety, the economy of the system must also be considered.

An electric locking system may be as simple as a single door lock or as complex as a multidoor system that includes some or all of the devices listed earlier. The system must coordinate all the electric equip-ment within it. Often, the locking system will also be required to interface with other equipment, such as fire or hazard detection sys-tem, X-ray machines, fans in air traps, and so on.

The electric lock offers a great deal of versatility in controlling an opening. Modes of control vary from system to system and may in-clude one or more of the following methods:

1. *Singular:* each door unlocked individually
2. *Simultaneous:* several doors unlocked at the same time by a single control
3. *Manual:* unlocking by personnel with key, card, or code
4. *Automatic:* unlocking by programmed time control
5. *Local:* on-site control at location of door
6. *Remote:* control at distance from door

7. *Programmed:* controls preprogrammed for unlocking and locking at specific times or during specific events (fire, hazard, etc.); controls programmed to provide interlock sequences
8. *Instant:* immediate locking or unlocking when control is activated
9. *Delayed:* preset time delay of locking or unlocking when control is activated

All of these modes can be individual or combined within a system. Today's computerized central control stations could combine all modes of control within a system. Features are often provided to give levels of authority to personnel who have access to the system. Cards or codes can be programmed to provide access to specific areas only or to specific areas only at certain times. Access authority can be changed at the computer whenever the need arises. Printouts can provide records of when an opening was used and who used it.

All functions available in a mechanical system are considerably broadened by electric locking. Thus, safety and security can be greatly improved by the use of electric security hardware.

FEATURES PROVIDED BY ELECTRIC LOCKING

The following chapters present detailed breakdowns and descriptions of electric locking devices and systems. First, however, let us study the qualities of electric locks and systems in general.

Versatility

Electric locks are available in many standard low voltages. Therefore, they can be interfaced with existing or new electronic equipment within a locking system. Other equipment that operates from or has control circuits that use low voltage may include automatic door operators, access control devices, and fire or hazard detection systems.

Electric locks operate in one of two modes: fail-safe or fail-secure. In the fail-safe mode, electric power must be applied constantly for the lock to remain locked. Loss of power to the lock will cause it to release and remain unlocked. The greatest advantage of this type of operation is that it can provide a means of immediate egress during a hazard or emergency. The lock, or zone of locks, can be released immediately when it is properly tied in with a local or central automatic hazard detection system. The term *fail-safe*, sometimes called *fail-open*, means exactly what it implies: a failure will cause a safe or open condition.

In the fail-secure mode, the lock does not require electric power to remain locked. When power is sent to the lock, it releases. In a power outage, there would be no way to release the lock without a manual override feature. This type of device is particularly useful in detention areas or places where security would be required during a power loss. The term *fail-secure*, sometimes called *fail-closed*, also means exactly what it implies: a failure will cause a secure or closed condition.

Reliability

Many electric locks have few moving parts; some have none. Maintenance and breakdowns are minimal on most devices. Manufacturers' warranties are generally very good. The operating life span of electromagnets may be considered indefinite.

Economy

The power use, or current draw, of most locking devices is normally very low. In a typical situation, ten electrical locks might draw no more current than a 60-watt light bulb. An electric locking system can substantially reduce the size of a costly, manned security force. The electric lock will work twenty-four hours a day, seven days a week, without supervision. A single guard at a central control station can control an entire system of doors.

Safety

The use of low-voltage, low-current locking devices at an opening provides electrical safety to the user of the system. Line power high voltage is commonly reduced to below 50 volts prior to being run to the locking device at the opening.

The safety of persons who are being protected by a security system is enhanced by the control and monitoring features provided by electric devices. The security status of an opening can be continuously reported and changed at any time. A tenant call system in an apartment complex is a prime example of these features. The tenant can monitor whether a main entrance is locked or unlocked and can allow or deny entrance to the building at will. Safety is further enhanced by the ability of selected doors to be unlocked automatically during an emergency.

Security

As already mentioned, the condition of an opening protected by an electric device can be monitored continuously. Features for reporting the locked or unlocked status of a device are available for all types of electric locks. The user can also determine whether a door is open or closed with other monitoring devices in the system. Control of a system of locks allows the lock status to be changed individually or as a group. These changes can be made instantaneously, by a single person, without the need to dispatch security guards to the openings. Automatic interlocks can also be programmed into the electronic security system.

Convenience

Doors protected by electric devices can be unlocked and opened with no more physical effort than the push of a button. This is especially desirable in systems designed for use by the aged or handicapped. Multiple doors in a system can be locked from a single control; it is not necessary to go to each opening.

Control

It should be evident by now that all sorts of controls are available for electric locking devices. The lock–unlock control of a device can be as simple as an ordinary wall switch, such as those used to turn lights on and off. The control may be a simple on-site pushbutton for unrestricted public use of an opening, or high-security devices, such as a fingerprint reader, may be used for controlled access or egress. Control may also be at a remote central station, where authorized personnel can control the use of hundreds of openings.

Today's electric locking and monitoring devices eliminate the need for a guard to patrol a building night and day to ensure security. One of the most desirable features of electric locking devices is the variety of monitoring options available. Solenoid-operated devices offer optional switches for positive monitoring of the bolt or keeper position.

These switches report the locked or unlocked status of the device. Electromagnets have built-in sensor switches to signal the secure or insecure condition of the lock.

Many locking devices also provide door status switches to monitor the actual door condition, open or closed. Antitamper switches are provided to monitor attempted violation of the lock itself. All of these options can be utilized for local or remote monitoring to facilitate control over the system.

Many of these options are used for additional control in systems such as "mantraps," equipment and door interlocks, and automatic doors. They may also be used to control other electrically operated devices within the system, such as fans and alarms.

Application

The uses of electric locking devices are limitless. Systems can vary according to the users' imaginations. Today's electronics and computerized systems offer a solution to any control problem that can arise. The degree of security achieved in a system depends on the type of lock used and the selection of other associated support equipment. Physically, locks are available for most door and frame conditions. Whether for new or retrofit construction, devices and accessories are available to accommodate nearly all conditions.

REVIEW

Compared to the 4,000-year history of mechanical locking, the electric locking industry is still in its adolescence. Most of the development of this industry has taken place within the past twenty to thirty years. The major growth has been in the past ten years, and the industry today offers unprecedented opportunities.

Ease of control, time savings, and enhancement of life safety and security systems have made electric locking very popular. Changes in criminal behavior have dictated changes in locking systems, and life safety and handicap codes have led to the development of new systems, made possible by electronic security devices.

Electronic security hardware includes not only locking devices but also door holders, exit devices, automatic door operators, and alarm and monitoring equipment. Some or all of these devices may be included in an electric locking system. The purpose of such a system is to authorize, restrict, or deny traffic within a specific area.

The electric lock offers many features and provides a great deal of versatility in systems design. Two advantages of electric locking rate high in comparison to mechanical locking: the cost is lower than guard service, and automatic control and monitoring assure that a system is performing as and when it should be.

2

The Basic Circuit

It is not necessary to be an electrical engineer to become involved in electronic security hardware. In everyday life, you use complex electronic equipment without becoming deeply involved in the engineering laws and formulas it took to develop the equipment. With relatively little training and some common sense, you are able to operate an automobile, a stereo system, and so forth. The same holds true for selling, selecting, installing, and maintaining electronic security products.

The intent of this chapter is to give the student who has no, or very little, electrical background a basic understanding of an electrical circuit. This understanding can then be related to a circuit or loop in a security or alarm system. Some electricians and electrical engineers may point out technical "inaccuracies" in such a presentation, but I have found it an ideal method to give hardwarepeople the basic information they will need to tackle a spec or installation they might otherwise have avoided. Architects, specifiers, hardware distributors, and anyone involved in electric hardware will benefit from this knowledge.

A SIMPLE CIRCUIT

The basic circuit is presented first in this book for a specific reason: to familiarize you with all the components necessary for a simple security system. Following chapters will analyze each component, in turn, and then Chapter 8 will return to complete systems. By then, you will have a better understanding of their operation.

A complete security system circuit can best be compared to the electric circuit in your own home. Most people are somewhat familiar with the circuit illustrated in Figure 2–1. Taking a few liberties, I will describe this simple circuit as having four components: (A) the appliance to be powered (load), (B) the power supply (power source), (C) the switch (control), and (D) the wiring (conductor).

Let us represent the load as a 100-watt light bulb, powered from a fused power source of 15-amp capacity. The control will be an ordinary on/off switch, and all components are wired together with 14-gauge wire.

When power is applied to the service panel, the bulb will illuminate, as the circuit is a completely closed loop. There is no break in the path, and the power will flow through the circuit. Operating the closed switch will create a break in the path and cause the bulb to go off.

The bulb is the load in the circuit and will draw only the amount of current it is designed to use. The load should be marked with its operating voltage and the amount of power it will consume. It may be marked in amps, which is the measure of current flow it will be drawing. Often, however, it will be marked in watts, which is a value used to indicate power consumed. In this book, you will be called upon to use very few formulas. One of the necessary formulas is for converting watts to amps. We have to convert watts to amps so that we are using the same units in which the power supply will be rated (amps). The

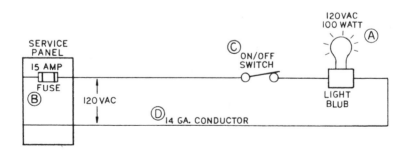

Figure 2–1.   Simple household circuit.

conversion is done by dividing watts by the operating voltage. For example, for an electric light bulb marked 120 VAC 100W:

$$\frac{100W}{120VAC} = 0.83 \text{ amp (current draw)}$$

A fuse is normally inserted in the circuit to prevent too much current draw due to excessive loads being added to the circuit. In the circuit in Figure 2–1, the light bulb is drawing only .83 amp. It is well below the 15 amps available and will operate without a problem.

Often the question will come up, "Won't 15 amps cause damage to a load that needs less amps?" The answer is no; a load will take only the amperage it is designed to use. The amperage that is left over is available for more loads that might be added to the circuit.

An example of an overloaded circuit is shown in Figure 2–2. To find the current value necessary to operate all the devices in this circuit, add their power ratings together. If all the devices were turned on at the same time, they would consume 2,150 watts. Using our formula, this can be changed to amps by dividing watts (2,150) by the operating voltage (120) to obtain 17.9 amps. We can see that using all the devices would exceed the 15 amps allowed by the fuse. This would cause an overload condition and blow the fuse. A blown fuse will open, similar to a switch opening, and break the circuit.

If the fuse were not in the circuit—or if someone "jumpered" it by crossing over it with a conductive material—several problems could

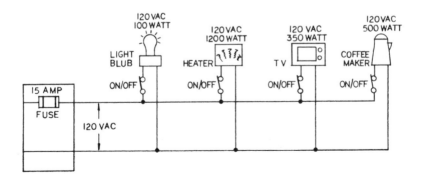

Figure 2–2. Overloaded circuit.

arise. The conductors (wires) making the circuit could become hot enough to melt its insulation and cause a fire. Excessive load could also damage the power supply if it were not able to supply the current called for.

It should be noted in Figure 2–2 that all devices in the circuit are labeled 120VAC. As will be discussed later, all components making up a circuit must be compatible. The load must be rated for the same voltage as the power source. If the power source output is 24VDC, then the load must be rated for the same voltage—that is, 24VDC. The fuse must be selected on the basis of the total load allowable on the circuit. Finally, the wiring and switches must be rated to handle the load power requirements.

BASIC ELECTRIC LOCKING CIRCUIT

Electronic security systems circuits are very similar in theory to the household circuit just discussed. The one big exception is that the high AC voltage is normally "stepped down" to a safer low AC voltage. Often, this low AC voltage is changed to DC voltage.

Although there are locking devices that operate from 120V, we will, for the most part, be examining low-voltage devices and systems throughout this text. By low voltages, I mean about 50 volts or less. The question of how much voltage can harm you will always prompt a lively discussion, with many different values tossed around. I believe it is correct to state, however, that 60 volts and under is perfectly safe and barely detectable to the touch.

The National Electrical Code, discussed in Appendix A, uses 50 volts as a sort of dividing line; most of the code is devoted to requirements for work above 50 volts. In UL 1034, Standard for Burglary Resistant Electric Locking Mechanisms, Underwriters Laboratories defines low voltage as not more than 30VAC or 42.4VDC. At any rate, you should develop the deepest respect for the high-voltage power source, which most often will be 120VAC.

A basic electric locking system consists of four components, as shown in Figure 2–3. The arrangement of these components, called a circuit, must include:

1. Load (electric locking device)
2. Power source (power supply, transformer, etc.)

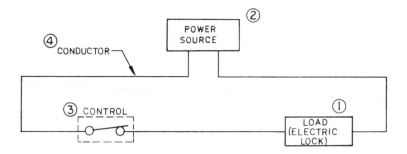

Figure 2–3. Electric locking circuit.

3. Control (on/off switch)
4. Conductor (wire run)

A fifth component, a monitoring device, may be added to the circuit. Monitoring devices are discussed in Chapter 7.

COMPONENTS OF AN ELECTRIC LOCKING CIRCUIT

Although each component of the electric locking circuit will be discussed in detail in Chapters 3 through 7, the following brief definitions will be useful.

Load

The load is the locking device itself, which uses electricity and converts this energy to magnetism. This magnetism is used to provide some form of physical door control, either through direct magnetic attraction, as in an electromagnetic lock, or through motion, as in a solenoid-operated lock. The device is designed to operate at a specific voltage, at which it will draw a specific current (amps).

The efficiency of the device is based on the percentage of electricity it uses to perform its primary purpose. An example of inefficiency would be heat from a light bulb. Inefficiency in a locking device will also be dissipated as heat. The three characteristics that may be known about a load are its operating voltage (E), the current (I) it uses at this voltage, and the resistance (R) it offers to the flow of current in the circuit. I have labeled these characteristics with the symbols E (voltage), I (current), and R (resistance) because these are the symbols used in the Ohm's law formulas (see Appendix F). The basic formula for Ohm's law is

$$I \text{ (amps)} = \frac{E \text{ (voltage)}}{R \text{ (resistance in ohms)}}$$

In this formula, the current is unknown and can be determined by dividing the known voltage by the known resistance. If the current and voltage are known, the resistance can be found by using the formula $R = E/I$. If the current and resistance are known, use the formula $E = IR$ to find the voltage. These formulas will come in handy for troubleshooting a locking device (see Chapter 9). If a monitoring device is in the circuit, it is an additional load, and the same rules apply.

Power Source

The power source is a power supply, transformer, battery, or the like, that provides the proper electrical energy to power the load. The power source output voltage must match the voltage required by the load. It must also be rated for enough power to operate the load. Usually, when calculating power requirements, you will be working with values measured in amps. Some power sources may be rated in volt/amps (VA), which can be converted to amps by dividing the rating by the output voltage. For example, for a transformer marked 24V 20VA on the output side:

$$\frac{20VA}{24V} = .83 \text{ amps (output power available)}$$

The power source may be selected to furnish either alternating current (AC) or direct current (DC). A transformer furnishes *only* AC current, and a battery furnishes *only* DC current.

Control

The control is a device that controls the flow or movement of electricity, permitting or preventing it from flowing through the circuit. It is commonly called a switch because it switches the electricity on or off. There are many types of controls with a wide range of functions.

A switch commonly has contacts that open or close to make or break a circuit. These contacts are rated to handle a maximum voltage and current.

Conductor

The conductor is the wire that ties all the components together in order to complete the circuit. The wire provides the path for the electricity to follow. It is affected by the voltage and current it must carry and the total length of wire run. The size (gauge) of wire and type of insulation is usually specified by the electrical contractor, but the basics of wire selection will be covered in Chapter 6.

MULTIPLE LOCKS IN A CIRCUIT

A circuit may include more than one locking device (and monitoring device) and more than one control, but it can have only one power supply, providing one voltage.

The circuit shown in Figure 2–4 has two locking devices, each labeled 24VDC, ¼ amp. The power supply must furnish 24VDC and a minimum of ½ amp. The ½ amp minimum rating is determined by

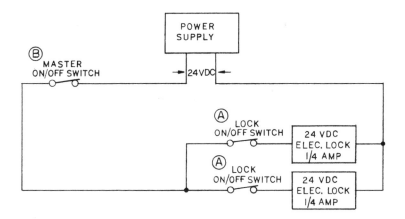

Figure 2–4.   Electric locking circuit with two locks.

adding together the current draw of all the loads in the circuit (¼ amp × 2). The power supply can be rated more than ½ amp without causing any problems.

The switches labeled (A) must be rated to carry at least ¼ amp, as that is the most current draw each will be required to carry. Switch (B), however, must be rated to carry at least ½ amp, as it will be required to carry the total current draw of both loads.

Following the current flow is like following a road map. In Figure 2–5, you can trace the path from one side of the power supply through the entire circuit to the other side of the power supply. You will see that there are two "roads" you can take, each constituting a separate, complete circuit.

Opening one of the (A) switches in Figure 2–4 would turn off the lock in its branch of the circuit. The other lock would continue to function, as a complete circuit would still exist all along its path. Note that opening the (B) switch would turn off both locks, as this would create a break in the main path that feeds the two branches.

This presentation of circuits provides the basics of a simple system. The next five chapters will present in-depth coverage of all the compo-

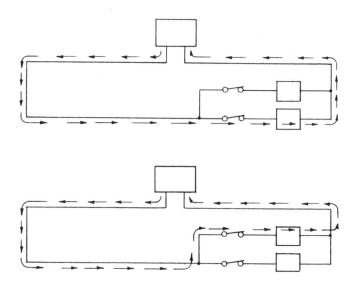

Figure 2–5.   Current flow through a circuit.

nents, and we will return to circuits and systems in Chapter 8. With the background you will gain in Chapters 3 through 7, circuits will make a lot more sense and building a system will become much easier.

REVIEW

A circuit must have four components:

1. Load
2. Power source
3. Control
4. Conductor

It may also have a fifth component—a monitoring device.

The circuit must be closed, or complete, for electricity to flow through it. A circuit may have more than one load in it, but all the loads in a circuit must operate at the same voltage. The total current draw of a circuit, measured in amps, is the sum of the current draw of all the loads in the circuit. The power source, control, and conductors are selected on the basis of the total load (current draw) on the circuit. The power source may be rated for a higher current output than the loads require, and a circuit may have more than one control. A fuse in the circuit will protect against circuit overload.

Voltage, measured in volts, is the force that drives the electricity through a circuit. For our purposes, we will consider 50 volts and under as low voltage. Current, measured in amps, is the amount of electricity that is available or actually flows through a circuit. Resistance, measured in ohms, is anything that offers opposition to the flow of current. *Watts* is a term used to express the rate of work or the power consumed: watts/voltage = amps. *Volt/amps* (VA) is a term used to express the measure of "apparent power" in AC circuits. For our purposes, we will convert to amps:

$$\frac{\text{VA (rating)}}{\text{V (output voltage)}} = \text{amps}$$

Ohm's law (see Appendix F) establishes the relationships between voltage, current (amps), and resistance. The basic Ohm's law formulas are as follows:

$$I \text{ (amps)} = \frac{E \text{ (voltage)}}{R \text{ (resistance)}}$$

$$R \text{ (resistance)} = \frac{E \text{ (voltage)}}{I \text{ (amps)}}$$

$$E \text{ (voltage)} = I \text{ (amps)} \times R \text{ (resistance)}$$

3

The Load

BASIC ELECTRIC LOCKING DEVICES

Electric locking devices fall into several basic categories that have these points in common:

1. They all operate at a specific voltage at which they draw a specific current.
2. The majority are available in standard low voltages, which are easily and safely interfaced with existing or added door equipment and power sources.
3. Most are available for both surface and mortise mounting, and many are produced for or adaptable to special mounting conditions.
4. All provide physical control of an opening (door, window, etc.).

Brief descriptions of each type of device will be followed by more comprehensive discussions. Several less popular and/or antiquated devices will not be covered here because their use in the security industry is not significant. It should also be noted that many devices are available in higher voltages, but because this text is primarily devoted to safer low-voltage systems, any mention of their availability will be only in passing.

Electromagnets

Electromagnets consist of two parts: the electromagnet, normally mounted on or in the door frame, and the strike plate or armature, which mounts on the door. When it makes contact with the magnet face, the armature secures the door by "bonding" with the magnetic field. Electromagnets require constantly applied electrical power to secure the door and will release whenever power is interrupted. This is considered the truest of the fail-safe locks, having no moving parts that could stick or bind during release.

Electric Strikes

The electric strike is an electrically operated mechanism for use with various standard latchbolt lock sets. The jamb-mounted device is used in place of the conventional lock strike plate. It provides the advantage of remote unlocking and relocking of the opening. Electric strikes are available as fail-safe or fail-secure and can be operated in a silent or an audible mode.

Solenoid-Operated Bolts

Solenoid-operated bolts are electrically operated deadbolts. They are available in a variety of mounting configurations in either fail-safe or fail-secure modes.

Solenoid-Operated Exit Devices

A solenoid-operated exit device is a panic device with a built-in solenoid for electrically retracting the latchbolt. It is a fail-secure unit in that interruption of power returns the latch bolt to a locked condition.

Electromechanical Devices

Electromechanical devices—such as a mortise or bored lockset—are specially designed to include a solenoid-operated mechanism for electric control. They are available in fail-safe or fail-secure modes. It is generally not a good idea to attempt to modify an existing mechanical lock to incorporate a solenoid. Mechanical locks were not designed for such operation, and adaptation to solenoid operation may cause many problems during usage.

ELECTROMAGNETISM

Since all the electric locking devices we will be describing use electromagnetism as their operating stimulus, a brief introduction to electromagnetism may help in understanding the operating principles of the devices.

A *magnet* is a body that has the property of attracting iron and steel. Some materials, when magnetized under the stimulation of a magnetic field, retain that magnetism when the exciting field has been removed; these are called *permanent magnets*. Materials that lose most of their magnetism when the exciting field has been removed are called *temporary magnets*. The temporary magnet is the basis for electric locking devices.

A wire shaped in the form of a helix, and carrying a current, will produce an intense magnetic field. This arrangement is called a *solenoid* or *electromagnet* (see Figure 3–1). Specially selected material inserted within the center of the helix will increase the available magnetic force. If the material within the coil is stationary, the unit will be an electromagnet; if the material is allowed to slide within the coil, the unit is called a solenoid. Figures 3–2 and 3–3 provide additional details of basic solenoids or electromagnets.

The area around an electromagnet where influence can be measured is called the *magnetic field*. The question often arises as to whether the magnetic field in a locking device is great enough to cause harm to computer tapes. I know of no circumstances in which such harm could be caused accidentally. The measurable magnetic field is usually less than an inch from the coil. Solenoid devices are usually mortised in headers and frames; when they are surface-mounted, they are encased in some sort of housing. It is doubtful that any appreciable magnetic field could be detected outside of these units. With electromagnets, the

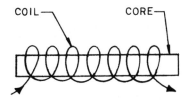

Figure 3–1. Simple solenoid or electromagnet.

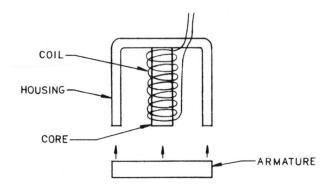

Figure 3–2. A fail-safe electromagnet requires power to hold the armature; with power loss, the armature falls away.

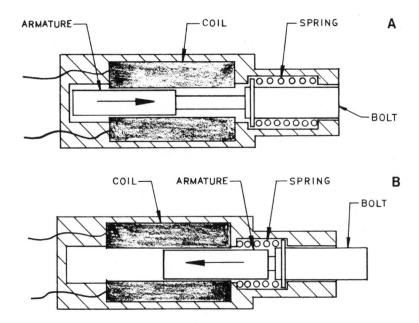

Figure 3–3. Solenoid-operated deadbolts. (A) A fail-safe unit (push solenoid) requires power to project the bolt; with power loss, the spring retracts the bolt. (B) A fail-secure unit (pull solenoid) requires power to retract the bolt; with power loss, the spring projects the bolt.

only way to harm computer tapes would be to place the tapes deliberately over the face of the magnet and energize the magnet. Normally, when a magnet is energized, the door is closed and the armature is in place, making it highly unlikely that any appreciable field would exist around the device. With the door open, the electromagnet either would be shut off or could be made to remain off through the use of a door status switch (discussed in a later chapter).

The strength of any device depends on the magnetic field strength, and the field being produced by the current flow through the coil depends on several factors: the size and number of turns of the wire in the coil, the characteristics of the core material, and the amount of current flowing. Generally, if the unit is properly designed, the larger it is, the stronger it will be.

Another factor that influences device strength is heat. During long periods of being energized, some units become quite heated. Operation of solenoids after prolonged energization may be noticeably sluggish, and overheated electromagnets will have a loss of holding force. These losses in strength are due to a weakened magnetic field, through loss of magnetic properties caused by heat. In properly designed units, heating is kept to a minimum. Where heating is unavoidable, other compensations are incorporated.

As noted earlier, with a loss of power, the magnetic field in electromagnets and solenoids collapses and the core material loses *most* of its magnetism. All magnetic materials used in core design do retain a certain amount of magnetism, called *residual magnetism*. In selecting core material, an effort is made to reduce this residual to its lowest level, while not sacrificing other important qualities. In solenoids, properly designed springs will overcome the residual without detrimental effects on the device operation. In electromagnets, which have no moving parts, other resources must be used to overcome any residual effect. Mechanical design and electric modules to reverse polarity are commonly used to nullify residual magnetism. These and other devices will be discussed in depth in the comprehensive study of each electromagnetic device.

SELECTION OF FEATURES

AC or DC

In selecting an electric locking device, a decision must be made regarding AC or DC operation. Normally, selection of component operating voltage is simply a matter of compatibility with the rest of the system. In terms of safety, when working with low voltages, AC is as safe as DC.

Most electromagnetic devices have coils that require DC voltage. The smooth, consistent flow of direct current results in a silent operating mode in continuous and intermittent duty devices. With electric strikes, where audible operation is sometimes desirable, alternating current operation causes vibration or "buzz" in the unit. In many instances, the device has a built-in rectifier that will allow the unit to be operated with either DC or AC input voltage.

Operating Mode

When selecting any electric locking device, the mode of operation should be one of the first considerations. The following definitions explain the terminology that will be used throughout this text when describing operating characteristics:

> *Continuous duty* rating should be specified for any solenoid-operated unit that must be energized for extended periods of time. It is normally available only in DC voltages. Some AC units may be adapted by adding an optional rectifier. Continuous duty rating is used, for example, in fail-safe units that are continuously energized.
>
> *Intermittent duty* rating may be used for any solenoid-operated unit that is energized for short periods of time. It is available in both AC and DC voltages. Intermittent duty rating is used, for example, in fail-secure units that are energized only briefly for unlocking cycles.
>
> *Fail-secure* mode is unlocked when energized, locked when de-energized (i.e., upon power failure). In electromagnets, which are by nature fail-safe, standby battery power is sometimes added to create a limited fail-secure condition.
>
> *Fail-safe* mode is locked when energized, unlocked when de-energized (i.e., upon power failure).
>
> *Fail-dormant* mode does not require energy to maintain a locked or unlocked state. When energized (intermittently), it will remain in either a locked or unlocked state until reenergized to change states. It is sometimes referred to as a "double-impulse" unit.

ELECTRIC STRIKES

Electric strikes are electromechanical units installed in the door frame in place of the conventional lock strike plate. Electric strikes are also available for mounting on the door frame. They are used in conjunction with various door lock sets to provide additional security features, including convenience and remote operation to lock or unlock doors electrically, controlling the egress and ingress of persons. Electric strikes are also known as electric door openers or electric releases.

Electric strikes use either a solenoid or an electromagnet to control a movable keeper. The keeper interfaces with the bolt of the lock device on the door. Electrical actuation of the strike allows opening of the door even though the bolt of the lock device is still extended. (See Figures 3–4 and 3–5.)

The strike operating mode may be either fail-secure or fail-safe. Fail-secure operation requires electrical actuation to release the keeper from its normally locked position. Loss of primary power would result in a locked condition; in the absence of emergency standby power, restoration of power would be necessary before the lock could be electrically released. Fail-safe operation requires constant electrical current to hold the keeper in the locked position. (The fail-safe strike is sometimes referred to as a reverse-action strike.) Interruption or loss of power releases the keeper, resulting in an unlocked condition. The fail-secure strike is the more popular unit.

The duty rating—either intermittent duty or continuous duty— must also be considered when selecting the operating mode. Intermittent duty may be used when the strike is energized only momentarily from time to time. Continuous duty should be selected for any strike that must be energized for extended periods of time.

Generally, fail-secure strikes may be intermittent duty except in rare circumstances where the strike must be energized (the door kept unlocked) for long periods. Unless the strike is so specified as standard, continuous duty may be an optional feature that must be specified when required. Fail-safe strikes are usually offered as an option. They are normally continuous duty rated, requiring constant electrical energy to remain locked.

Voltage selection is another factor to be considered in specifying an electric strike. Since electric strikes are available in a wide variety of AC and DC voltages, several points must be considered in making this selection.

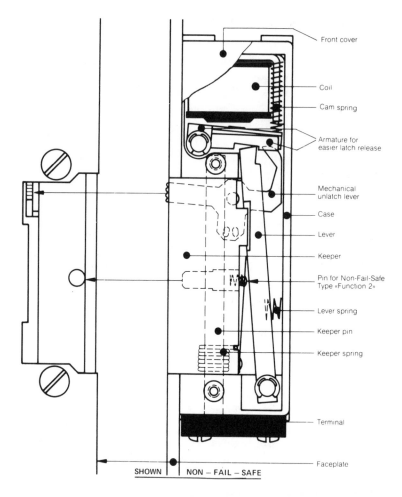

Figure 3–4. Cutaway view of an electric strike. (Courtesy of Rofu International Corp.)

When activated by AC voltage, the strike will emit a buzzing sound. This sound is inherent in *all* AC-activated strikes. It is usually not considered offensive in intermittent use and acts as an audible signal that the door lock has been released. The fail-secure, intermittent duty, 24VAC strike is probably the most commonly used unit today.

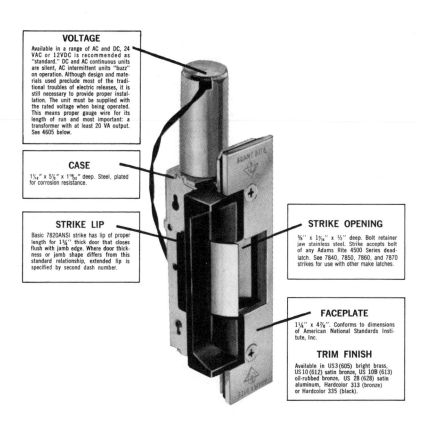

VOLTAGE
Available in a range of AC and DC, 24 VAC or 12VDC is recommended as "standard." DC and AC continuous units are silent, AC intermittent units "buzz" on operation. Although design and materials used preclude most of the traditional troubles of electric releases, it is still necessary to provide proper installation. The unit must be supplied with the rated voltage when being operated. This means proper gauge wire for its length of run and most important: a transformer with at least 20 VA output. See 4605 below.

CASE
1½₆" x 5½" x 1¹⁵⁄₃₂" deep. Steel, plated for corrosion resistance.

STRIKE LIP
Basic 7820ANSI strike has lip of proper length for 1¾" thick door that closes flush with jamb edge. Where door thickness or jamb shape differs from this standard relationship, extended lip is specified by second dash number.

STRIKE OPENING
⅝" x 1⁷⁄₁₆" x ½" deep. Bolt retainer jaw stainless steel. Strike accepts bolt of any Adams Rite 4500 Series deadlatch. See 7840, 7850, 7860, and 7870 strikes for use with other make latches.

FACEPLATE
1¼" x 4⅞". Conforms to dimensions of American National Standards Institute, Inc.

TRIM FINISH
Available in US3 (605) bright brass, US 10 (612) satin bronze, US 10B (613) oil-rubbed bronze, US 28 (628) satin aluminum, Hardcolor 313 (bronze) or Hardcolor 335 (black).

Figure 3–5. Components of an electric strike. (Courtesy of Adams Rite Mfg. Co.)

If silent operation is desired, DC voltage may be specified or a rectifier may be added to the AC circuit. Some units are available with a built-in rectifier and use either AC or DC current. Their operation is always silent.

Normally, the electrical circuit is designed to be compatible with the selected strike. In some cases, existing circuits must be used and the strike must be selected to match them. An example of this would be the 48VDC circuit used by most telephone companies.

Most manufacturers' catalogs list the current requirements of their units—usually as a single value that can be used when selecting the power supply or calculating system current requirements. Occasionally, units are listed with two values, inrush current and hold current. Inrush current may also be specified as peak instantaneous current. Hold current may be called seated current or continuous current. As may be surmised from their names, inrush current is the higher, short-duration current needed to start the unit, and hold current is the lower, continuous current needed to keep the unit in its required mode while energized. The selected power supply must be able to handle the inrush load requirements to operate the unit properly.

Many strikes are available with optional built-in monitoring switches. These switches are used for remote monitoring of the strike and lockbolt status and for creating interlock systems. Generally, one- or two-switch options are offered; selection is based on system requirements.

Most common is the two-switch option, whereby one switch is activated by the strike locking cam or solenoid plunger that controls the strike keeper and the other switch is activated by the lockbolt's penetration into the strike. The switches indicate that the strike is locked and the lockbolt is properly seated. Both conditions must exist to obtain a "secure" indication.

In some cases, when the door is open, the switch actuators may be manually depressed, giving a false "secure" indication at the monitor. Adding a separate, concealed door status switch, wired in series with the strike switches, can help overcome this problem. In this situation, three separate conditions must be met to cause a "secure" indication: (1) strike in locked position, (2) lockbolt seated, and (3) door closed.

In relation to other electric security devices, several points may be considered weaknesses in electric strike usage, depending on the degree of security desired, cost limitations, and adaptability to existing conditions. They may or may not be factors to consider in selecting electric strikes as the proper security device in a system or application:

Vulnerability to tampering: Unlike other locking devices, strike applications often offer double pick points—the strike itself and the lock device on the door.

Lack of versatility: Uses are limited to jamb mounting in conjunction with door-mounted lock devices.

Critical alignment: Mounting is somewhat critical in interfacing with the lock device on the door.

The electric strike, as described, is commonly used for low-security traffic-control situations. Probably the most commonly recognized use is for apartment entrance doors and bank interior doors, where audio or visual contact is first made with the person desiring entrance, who is then "buzzed" in from a remote location by actuation of the strike release.

Not generally considered high-security devices, electric strikes are used for interior and perimeter door control, stairwell or elevator door control, fire exits, and interlock door control.

Several electric strike characteristics, options, and uses are commonly available throughout the industry. Some features are standard, some are optional, and a great variety of devices and styles are available. Manufacturers' literature should be consulted for availability of desired features.

Voltages

Selection of operating voltage requires consideration of the following characteristics.

- *DC input* must be operated from a DC power source only. If AC power of matching voltage is present, a rectifier must be placed between power source and the strike to convert AC to DC. DC operation is always silent.
- *AC input* must be operated from an AC power source only. AC operation is audible. Some units will accept an optional rectifier for silent operation.
- *AC/DC input* is internally rectified and will operate from either AC or DC voltage. Operation is always silent.

As shown in the following table, there is a wide range of available voltages. When selecting the voltage of the strike you require, consider the voltage of other equipment in the system, the voltage of the power source if it is specified or existing, the current draw, and the available voltages for the type of unit you have selected.

Dual	AC	DC	AC/DC
3–6VDC/8–16VAC	12	6	8
6VDC/12VAC	16	12	12
12VDC/24VAC	24	24	24
48VDC/115VAC	48	48	48
	115	115	

Operating Modes

Several operating function options are part of the electric strike selection process:

- Silent or audible
- Fail-safe or fail-secure
- Continuous duty or intermittent duty

Options

Some of the more commonly available options for electric strikes are as follows:

- Architectural finishes
- Mortar guards and connector boxes
- Mounting tabs
- Monitoring switches
- Resistor (for line supervision security systems)
- Rectifier
- Extended strike lip (for nonstandard door thickness or jamb shape)
- Secondary keeper spring to engage deadlocking lever on dead-latching locksets
- Lock guard

Mounting

Many mounting variables are encountered in electric strike installation. The market today offers electric strikes that can be adapted to the following devices and conditions:

Lock Devices
- Key in knob latchset
- Deadbolt lock
- Rim lock with latchbolt
- Mortise and cylindrical locks
- Mortise entrance lock with latchbolt
- Mortise latch lock, cylindrical lock and mortise panic exit device— with or without auxiliary deadlock latch
- Unit lock

Frame Conditions
- Mortise and surface mounting
- Left- or right-handed strikes, some reversible
- Standard ANSI cutout strike fronts
- Wood, aluminum, and hollow metal jambs

Door Conditions
- In-swinging doors
- Out-swinging doors
- Sliding doors
- Two-way swinging doors

Listing

Many strikes are available with Underwriters Laboratories (UL) Fire Door and Burglary listing.

Maintenance

Preventive maintenance should be performed semiannually to minimize service problems. Cleaning and lubrication may be required more frequently on high-usage installations or in dirty environments. The following maintenance procedures will help keep the unit functional and trouble-free:

- Keep mechanism free of foreign matter.
- Never operate at higher than specified voltages.
- Check that all mounting and assembly screws are secure.
- Check for alignment with locking device.
- Check for binding between faceplate and keeper.

Units are normally factory lubricated. If necessary, when the unit is disassembled, pivot points may be lightly lubricated with molybdenum disulfide or graphite. It is best not to lubricate an installed unit in an attempt to solve poor operation. Troubleshoot and consult the installer or manufacturer if you cannot identify the problem.

Troubleshooting

Weak or sluggish action is usually an electrical problem. The first check to make will require using your meter (see Chapter 9). Measure the voltage at the unit with the unit energized. If the voltage is lower than specified, the problem may be an undercapacity transformer if the wire run is short. With long wire runs, it may be a voltage drop due to wire of insufficient gauge. If they are known, check the current draw and resistance of the unit. Variations here could indicate a defective unit.

A keeper that does not respond when energized may be an internal mechanical problem. Double-check your wiring hookup to be sure that the unit is receiving the voltage. (See Figure 3–6.)

SOLENOID-OPERATED DEADBOLTS

Electromechanical devices incorporating a solenoid-driven deadbolt are available in a great variety of shapes and sizes. They run from low- to high-security devices and cover a wide range of mounting requirements. Unlike electric strikes, they need no other mechanical lock device to provide security. They combine the advantages of remote electric control and almost unlimited versatility with relatively economical cost. Solenoid-operated deadbolts are also known as electric locks, power bolts, and electric deadbolts (see Figure 3–7).

Units usually consist of a solenoid, a bolt assembly, a lock front or housing, and a mating strike plate or block. The lock may be mounted to or in the door frame or, in some cases, to or in the door itself. When energized, the device locks or unlocks by moving a deadbolt in or out of a mating strike.

The operating mode may be either fail-secure or fail-safe, much as described in the discussion of electric strikes. The bolt assembly invariably uses some type of spring return mechanism. The fail-secure device has a normally projected bolt. When energized, the bolt retracts

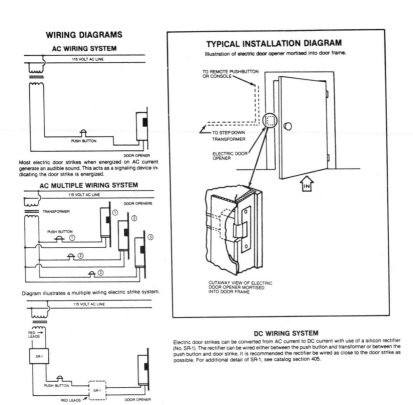

Figure 3–6. Typical installation details for an electric strike. (Courtesy of Trine Products Corp.)

to unlock and loads the spring mechanism. Interruption of power releases the solenoid and allows the spring to return the bolt to its normally projected state. The fail-safe device has a normally retracted bolt. When energized, the bolt projects to lock and loads the spring mechanism. Interruption of power releases the solenoid and allows the spring to return the bolt to its normally retracted state. Both operating modes are equally popular because of the great variety of applications for this type of electric lock.

The duty rating may be either intermittent or continuous duty. This is not normally a selection factor, however, as most electric deadbolts are built with a continuous heavy-duty solenoid.

Figure 3–7. Mortise-mount right-angle electric bolt. (Courtesy of Locknetics Security Products)

A less conventional unit, sometimes called the fail-dormant or double-impulse lock, is found in limited use today. It is an electric lock with two solenoids that require intermittent energizing to change states. It will remain in a locked or unlocked state without applied energy. Intermittently applied energy changes it from one state to the other. This type of lock is a high-security device for use in detention areas, prisons, banks, and other high-security areas.

Solenoid-operated deadbolts are not offered in as wide a voltage range as electric strikes. Because they are heavier duty devices, the lower-range voltages are not available. They are normally available as 12VAC, 24VAC, 115VAC, 12VDC, and 24VDC units; 24VAC is the most popular.

The standard operation of these units is silent, regardless of AC or DC input. The coil of the solenoid is a basic DC coil, which operates silently. It may have an internal rectifier to adapt it to AC input. Units operated from AC only are designed with a "shorted turn" around part of the coil's magnetic circuit to ensure smooth, silent operation.

When selecting the power supply or calculating system current requirements, the same points hold true as those outlined for electric strikes. Although most units will be specified with a single value for current draw, you will occasionally find units listed with two values—inrush current and hold current. For a dual-solenoid (double-impulse) unit, there will be separate current values for each solenoid. In any case, the power supply must be able to handle the highest current value to operate the unit properly.

Many electric bolts are available with built-in door status or strike monitoring switches. These switches—also referred to as jamb switches and relock switches—are variously found as standard or optional, depending on the manufacturer. They are used in series with the electric lock to prevent premature throwing of the bolt. They keep the bolt retracted until the door is in a closed position. The door status switch is also used to coordinate multidoor interlock systems.

Another commonly available switch option is the bolt position switch. It is located within the lock device to monitor the actual position of the bolt—that is, fully projected or fully retracted. It may be used remotely to monitor the true position of the bolt and can be used in conjunction with the door status switch to indicate a secure condition. This switch is also used for interfacing with automatic door equipment by providing a signal to the door operator equipment. If the bolt is projected, the switch provides an open circuit in the door operator control circuit, disabling the operator. Until a retracted bolt provides a closed circuit, the door operator will not function.

Advantages and Disadvantages

The following are general comparisons between the electric deadbolt and other devices.

Relative to an Electric Strike
- *More secure:* It is considered a security lock itself, as opposed to an electric control of a mechanical lock.
- *More costly:* It is basically more expensive than a strike, unless you also consider the cost of the mechanical lock used with the strike.
- *Poorer emergency egress* (fail-secure condition): An electric strike may allow mechanical means of egress through the use of certain types of latch sets associated with it. Most common electric deadbolts provide no mechanical means for emergency egress. (*Note:* A few units are available with mechanical release options.)

Relative to an Electromagnet
- *Less secure:* The breakthrough area of the electric bolt is limited to a small area where forces can be applied. It can be violated by ripping the strike off or out of the door or by prying the door away from the frame and slipping the bolt out of the strike.
- *Less costly:* The electric bolt is normally less expensive than the electromagnet.
- *Poorer emergency egress* (fail-safe condition): Even as an electrically fail-safe unit, mechanical parts that can stick and bind make it far less fail-safe than an electromagnet, which has no moving parts. Electric deadbolts are not compatible with panic bar switch releases. Pushing the bar to electrically release the bolt also simultaneously causes the bolt to jam against the strike and not retract.
- *Poorer durability:* The life of an electric deadbolt is limited by the wear and failure rate of its mechanical parts.

General
- Fail-secure electric bolt use should be limited to nonpublic areas, where life safety will not be compromised.
- Electric bolts are not recommended where panic bar release hardware is the only means of egress.

Applications

The electric deadbolt, as described, is used in a variety of ways. It is generally recognized as a medium-security device, although high-security devices are available. Its use in traffic control situations, especially interlock systems, is very popular. The versatility of the units available today makes it suitable as a general-purpose lock, not limited to doors.

The following list of popular applications of the electric deadbolt, though lengthy, does not by any means cover all the uses of this device:

- Doors to money-counting rooms in banks
- Bathroom interlocks in hospitals, nursing homes, dormitories, schools
- Entrance doors in office buildings, lobbies, laundromats, post offices, hospitals, schools, public areas
- Interlocks for X-ray equipment and other dangerous equipment
- Exit doors, with approved emergency releases, in hospitals, sanitariums, children's homes
- Special and custom applications, not limited to doors
- Doors to tool rooms and test areas in industrial buildings
- Power and machine enclosures
- Safety interlocks for darkrooms, clean rooms, air showers
- Security interlocks in high-security areas, computer rooms
- Special interlocks for unlimited quantity and sequencing of doors (requires logic controller)
- Doors to loading docks, incinerator areas, high-theft storage areas in supermarkets
- Doors to waiting rooms, reception areas, hotel/motel lobbies

Several electric deadbolt characteristics, options, and uses are commonly available throughout the industry. Some features are standard, some are optional, and a great variety of devices and styles are available. Manufacturers' literature should be consulted for availability of desired features.

Voltages

The following table presents the available voltages for electric deadbolts:

AC	DC	AC/DC
12	12	12
24	24	24
115		

Operating Modes

The following operating modes are available for electric deadbolts:

- Fail-safe
- Fail-secure
- Silent
- Continuous duty

Bolt Sizes

The following table presents the commonly available bolt sizes:

Bolt Diameter	Throw
1/2"	1/2"
5/8"	1/2"
5/8"	3/4"
3/4"	3/4"
13/16"	1/2"

Options

Some of the more commonly available options for electric deadbolts are as follows:

- Architectural finishes
- Adjustable time delay
- Bolt position switch
- Door status switch (or strike switch or automatic relock switch)
- Emergency release
- Indicator lights
- Lock front—fixed or adjustable
- Lock box—jamb-mounted/mortised
- Mounting tabs
- Strikes—mortised or surface

Mounting

The variety of mounting methods is almost endless in electric deadbolt application. Units have been mounted almost everywhere on door frames or doors.

Frame Conditions
- Right-angle bolts for narrow frame conditions
- Bolt can project in any plane
- Mortise mounting
- Surface mounting
- A variety of strikes to satisfy almost all installation needs

Door Conditions
- Chain link or tubular steel gates (swinging or sliding)
- In-swinging doors
- Out-swinging doors
- Overhead doors
- Roll-up doors
- Sliding doors

(*Note:* Electric bolts are also available for doors equipped with panic devices with top latchbolts.)

Maintenance

Although only minimal maintenance can be performed on electric deadbolts, several points should be checked periodically to minimize service problems:

- Keep mechanism free of foreign matter.
- Never operate at higher than specified voltages.
- Check that all mounting and assembly screws are secure.
- Check alignment of bolt and strike opening.
- Lubrication is not advised. Some units have self-lubricating bearings. If unit operates poorly, troubleshoot and consult the installer or manufacturer if the problem cannot be identified.

Troubleshooting

Weak or sluggish action is usually an electrical problem. The first check to make will require using your meter (see Chapter 9). Measure the voltage at the unit with the unit energized. If the voltage is lower than specified, the problem may be an undercapacity transformer if the wire run is short. With long wire runs, it may be a voltage drop due to wire of insufficient gauge. If they are known, check the current

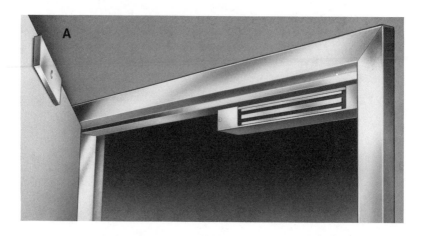

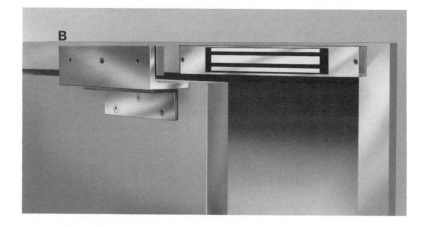

draw and resistance of the unit. Variations here could indicate a defective unit.

Electric deadbolts can run very hot if they are energized for long periods of time. Usually, metal frames and the air space around the solenoid area will dissipate some of the heat. In wood frames, hot solenoids have been known to scorch the wood. Allow air space if possible, or insulate the area around the solenoid.

A bolt that fails to respond when the unit is energized may be an internal mechanical problem. Double-check your wiring hookup to be sure the unit is receiving the correct voltage.

C

Figure 3-8. Electromagnets for (A) out-swinging doors, (B) in-swinging doors, and (C) sliding doors. (Courtesy of Locknetics Security Products)

ELECTROMAGNETS

Compared to the other electric locking devices, the electromagnetic lock is the "youngster" of the family. Its chief distinction in this family is that no moving parts are involved in its operation. This feature results in a highly reliable, long-life unit. It also makes it the truest of the fail-safe units, because it has no mechanism that can cause sticking or binding. Electromagnets are generally categorized as high-security locks and are available in a good range of mounting styles (see Figure 3-8). Although they are more costly than other types of devices, they are a better choice in many cases. Their merit has gained wide recognition and they are rapidly becoming more popular. Electromagnetic locks, also called magnetic door locks, are often identified by trade names assigned by the manufacturers.

Magnetic locks consist of two components—neither of which has any moving mechanisms—which are called the electromagnet and the armature, or strike plate. The electromagnet is usually mounted on the door frame and the armature is mounted on the door (see Figures 3–9 and 3–10). When the door is closed, the armature must be centered over and in contact with the face of the magnet. When the magnet is energized, the magnetic field that is produced attracts the armature and creates a bond between the two parts of the lock. The strength of the bond is defined by the holding force rating of the lock.

The magnet portion of the lock operates through a magnetic field produced by electrical energy. The advantage of this is that, unlike a permanent magnet, the magnetic field can be turned on and off by controlling the electric power.

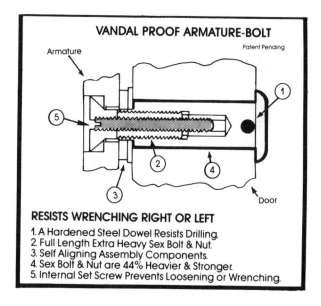

Figure 3–9. Armature mounting hardware. (Courtesy of Magnegard Division)

The first magnets were produced by ganging several small coils of wire with solid cores in a series circuit. The resulting magnets exhibited holding forces ranging from 400 to 800 pounds. As technology advanced the design of electromagnetic locks, one-piece rectangular coils replaced the pole-type magnet.

Today's magnet consists of a continuous, insulated copper wire, wound in many turns around the center section of a rectangular, E-shaped frame. The coil portion is encapsulated in an epoxy compound. The epoxy cures into an electrically insulated material that does not generally support combustion and is resistant to chemicals and other fluids. This material serves as both a sealant and a structural member of the magnet.

The frame material and shape are designed for optimum results as an electromagnet. As mentioned earlier, all magnetic material will retain some magnetism after it is deenergized. Magnetic materials selected for electromagnetic locks exhibit very low magnetic retentivity, or residual magnetism, when the current is switched off. In most cases, the residual magnetism is so low that it is barely noticeable when the unit is mounted. In cases where residual magnetism is higher than desired, some manufacturers offer electronic modules to remove this effect when the magnet is deenergized.

The shape of the frame tends to concentrate the magnetic field in a localized area, which enhances the strength of the magnetic field. All these design improvements produce much higher holding forces and less power consumption in approximately the same size package as the earlier locks.

Another design improvement involves temperature rise. Earlier locks produced a fair amount of heat, since electrical energy applied to the coil is dissipated as heat. No energy is used for mechanical work, since the lock is a static force that does not exert any motion. Later, more efficient units show much less temperature rise. Generally, it rises approximately 30°F above an ambient temperature of 68°F measured during a bench test. In actual mounted conditions, most of this heat is dissipated through the frame. The lower the heat rise, the stronger the magnetic field.

The armature, though normally made of common steel, is designed to complement the magnet. It is sized specifically to provide a certain mass that interacts with the magnetic field. It is for this reason that "homemade" armatures should not be used, as it is doubtful that they

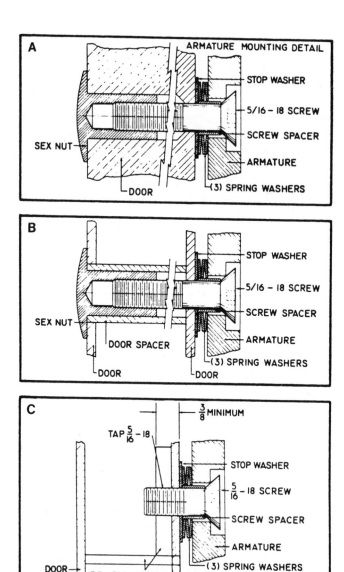

Figure 3–10. Mounting hardware. (A) Through bolt, solid door. (B) Through bolt, hollow door. (C) Direct mount, hollow door. (D) Angle bracket

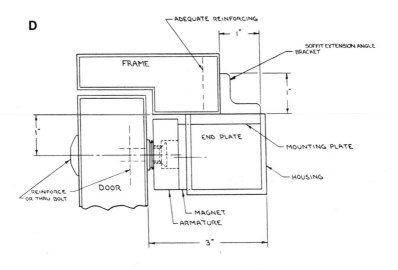

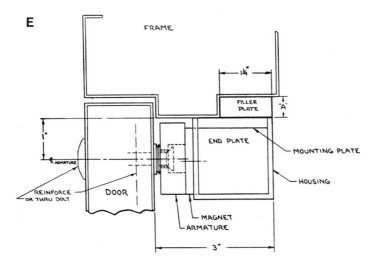

to extend soffit. (E) Filler plate to extend stop. (Courtesy of Locknetics Security Products)

would produce the holding force for which the magnet and armature set is rated.

A question that always arises is whether there is a significant magnetic field external to the magnet. This is usually brought up in regard to the effect of the magnetic field on computer tapes or on delicate electronic instruments. Tests have shown that the magnetic flux field is negligible beyond one inch from the magnet.

The electromagnet is available in several styles of housing for surface and mortised mounting. Holding forces of 1,000 to 1,200 pounds are considered adequate for most standard security doors. Some higher-rated units are available, but their use on standard doors could be considered overkill. The forces needed to violate a 1,000-pound magnet would most likely destroy the door and/or the frame before parting the bond between a properly mounted magnet and armature.

Smaller units, with about 500 pounds holding force, are used in sliding door applications and traffic control situations. They are adequate for interior doors where high security is not the prime consideration. They have also been used as door holders. Conventional magnetic door holders are usually rated around 40 pounds holding force. They hold the door in an open position until the electromagnet is released by a fire panel or similar alarm station. In some instances— such as in high schools and detention centers—there is a problem of the doors being forced manually from the door holder. A 500-pound holding force magnetic lock used as a holder certainly ends that problem!

The electromagnet is normally mounted in such a manner that the armature is pulling directly away from the magnet. In a direct-shear situation, where the armature is being slid off the face of the magnet, up to 80 percent of the holding force will be lost. A weak header or frame can cause a partial-shear condition, wherein the armature, when being pulled away from the magnet, will start to slide down the face of the magnet. This condition will result in a weaker than rated holding force. Some units are available with an antishear pin on the face of the magnet to help prevent this condition. These magnets are mortise-mounted, resulting in a totally concealed lock, thus preserving the aesthetic appearance of the opening (e.g., for a revolving door or decorative entrance).

A reduction in holding force can also result when there is foreign matter between the magnet and armature mating surfaces. Anything that introduces an air gap, however small, will reduce the bond.

The magnetic lock operating mode is always fail-safe. Whenever power is interrupted or lost, the magnet will release. The lack of any moving mechanism means that no secondary operation, such as a spring return bolt, is necessary to release the door when power is removed. Adding an emergency battery standby power system does not make the unit fail-secure. It will still release when the standby power is expended. Standby power is used only to prolong a locked status until primary power can be restored.

Unlike electromechanical devices, electromagnets require no duty rating. The magnetic lock, when energized, will operate without trouble continuously. It can operate at up to 50 percent over rated voltage without failure. A voltage drop of over 10 percent of rated voltage will cause a significant loss of holding force. Some units are designed to allow for voltage adjustment options, which can vary the holding force for special applications.

Electromagnets are normally offered only for 12VDC and 24VDC operation. A built-in rectifier is a common option, allowing 12VAC or 24VAC operation. The latest generation of magnets draw very little current, regardless of holding force rating. Ordinarily, current ratings run from ¼ to ½ amp. When electromagnets are used in a circuit, other components must be protected from voltage spike. When the electromagnet is switched off, a brief voltage spike or back voltage is generated from the collapsing magnetic field. This spike can damage solid state devices, lamps, relay contacts, and other components of the circuit. The spike can be suppressed by placing a diode or metal oxide varistor (MOV) across the leads of the magnet between the magnet and the system components. Heavy-duty switches in the circuit can withstand the spike, but it will lead to shorter switch contact life. The use of a diode or rectifier bridge at the lock may cause a slight delay in the release of the magnet, but it is usually not appreciable.

Magnetic locks are available with a variety of monitoring switches and sensors. Built-in door status switches are a common option on surface-mounted units. They may be used for door status indication, in series with the magnet to keep power off while the door is open, or to set up interlock systems. Antitamper switches are available to signal any attempt to remove the magnet housing. Some manufacturers offer built-in sensors to monitor power and/or bond conditions of the lock.

Power sensors indicate the actual energized or unenergized state of the lock. Bond sensors confirm proper armature contact (efficient bond) and will indicate a loss of holding force due to improper armature contact or critical voltage drop.

Compared to electric strikes and solenoid bolts, about the only negative feature of the electromagnet would be its higher cost. This is offset, however, by the desirable features it offers, which include the following:

- It is considered the most secure device.
- Its unique design makes it the most fail-safe device. This allows it to be adapted to situations involving strict adherence to life/safety codes.
- Its lack of moving parts and the minimal effect of overvoltage on it make it a very durable unit.
- Maintenance is minimal.
- It is more adaptable to poorly fitted or poorly hung doors.

Applications

The electromagnet can be used almost anywhere. Although it is primarily for ordinary indoor use, it has been used successfully in many outside applications. When shielded from the worst weather, the unit tends to keep itself dry and ice-free by its own warmth. If it is constantly energized, its temperature will rise approximately 30°F over ambient temperatures.

This type of lock has also been used in many applications other than doors—from desk drawer locks to machinery hold-down pads.

Because the electromagnet is truly fail-safe, it is used extensively on doors with panic device releases. If loss of security due to power loss is a consideration, battery standby power can be utilized. The lock can still be tied into a fire panel system to ensure immediate release upon an alarm signal. Because there are no moving parts to hinder its release, the magnet is winning increasing approval for use on fire exit doors. The NFPA Life Safety Codes cover this type of lock and even approve of a delayed egress system with certain qualifications. This system is becoming very popular with airports, chain stores, institutions, and many other security-oriented users.

At holding force ratings of 1,000 pounds and higher, it is considered a high-security device. Electromagnets with lower holding forces are commonly used for interior door traffic control situations. Low holding force magnets have also been used on aluminum store-front doors, because it is unlikely that anyone could violate the lock without first destroying the frame or glass.

Magnetic locks are also available for reinforced steel attack and blast doors. The locks have about 3,000 pounds holding force and provide security where intruders are expected to use other equipment to aid in gaining entry.

The versatility of the electromagnet allows its use in any of the applications listed for the electric strike and the electric bolt, although its higher cost usually limits its use to high-security requirements. Although it is not considered a detention hardware item, it would be ideal in many prison and detention facilities. A partial list of some of the places electromagnets have been used includes the following:

Institutions	Jewelry stores
Correction centers	Computer centers
Psychiatric wards	Libraries
Hospitals	Airports
Laboratories	Department stores
Banks	Courtroom areas
Schools	Recreation complexes

Several electromagnet characteristics, options, and uses are commonly available throughout the industry. Some features are standard, some are optional, and a great variety of devices and styles are available. Manufacturers' literature should be consulted for availability of desired features.

Voltages

The following table presents the available voltages for electromagnets:

AC	DC
12	12
24	24

Operating Modes

The following operating modes are standard for electromagnets:

- Fail-safe
- Silent
- Continuous duty

Holding Force

Electromagnets are available with holding forces ranging from 500 to 3,000 pounds.

Options

Some of the more commonly available options for electromagnets are as follows:

- Architectural finishes
- Adjustable time delay
- Magnetic bond sensor
- Door status switch
- Indicator lights
- Rectifier bridge
- Adjustable holding force
- Custom-length housings
- Antitamper switches
- All glass door adapters
- Guard plates

Mounting

The electromagnet is generally surface-mounted, with the armature pulling directly away from the face of the magnet. On out-swinging doors, the magnet is normally mounted on the doorstop surface under the header, as close to the strike jamb as possible (see Figure 3–11). The closer the magnet is moved to the hinge side, the less the holding force. This is caused by the leverage that is gained as the centerline of the magnet moves farther away from the centerline of the doorknob or pull plate.

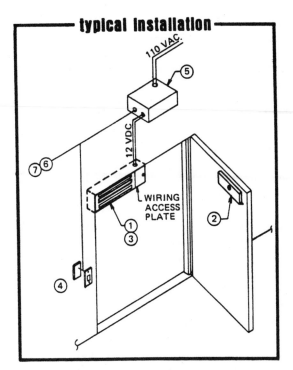

typical installation

1. Model #3900 Electric Lock
2. Electric Lock Armature
3. Door Status Switch Optional*
4. Local On/Off Station Controls
5. Power Supply
6. Remote On/Off Station Controls*
7. Hazard Sensing Safety Devices*

*As System Requires

Figure 3–11. Electromagnet installation diagram. (Courtesy of Security Engineering, Inc.)

It is very unlikely that anyone could pull open a door with a 1,000-pound (or more) magnet mounted at the top. The biggest complaint about this method of locking comes from detention facilities. The complaint is not that the lock does not hold, but that it holds so well that repeated attempts to violate the lock cause bending and distortion of the door. Probably the only answer to this complaint is to mount a double magnet vertically along the strike jamb of the frame. When locked, it would be virtually impossible to rack the door.

Pairs of out-swinging doors with a center mullion would need two single magnetic locks. If the opening has no center mullion, a double magnetic lock in a common housing may be used. For situations where high security is not needed, a single magnet with two small armatures is available. The lock would be centered between the doors and an armature mounted to each leaf. The holding force for each leaf would be half the rated holding force of the lock less 10 to 20 percent for efficiency losses.

In-swinging doors usually require that the lock be on the pull side of the door. There are locks available that mount to the face of the frame header and are supplied with a special bracket to mount the armature to the door. Other applications of the magnetic lock—for example, on wire mesh gates or chain link gates—usually require some customized hardware to accomplish proper mounting.

One of the best features of this type of lock is its tolerance of misalignment between the door and the frame. Unlike the electric strike and the solenoid bolt, it will grab the armature plate even when it is out of alignment. Of course, there are limitations to how much mismatch there can be, but generally, the lock will still provide a healthy holding force at ⅛ to ¼ inch out of alignment.

Electromagnets are applicable to the following door conditions:

- Out-swinging doors
- In-swinging doors
- Sliding doors

Also, with custom mounting, they can be adapted to almost any door condition, including gates, roll-up doors, and so on.

Maintenance

Because it has no moving parts, the electromagnet requires very little maintenance. It is recommended that the mating faces of the magnet and armature be checked for cleanliness every six months or so. They should be free of any foreign matter, including paint. These surfaces may be cleaned with a nonabrasive cleaning pad. Wiping the surfaces with an oil-dampened cloth will help protect the surface finish, especially in corrosive or humid atmospheres.

The mounting hardware should be checked to ensure that the magnet and armature are properly mounted. In most cases, the armature should be free to "float" or pivot slightly. A weakened header or a sagging door could cause misalignment of the mating faces and should be corrected.

Troubleshooting

There is very little that can go wrong with an electromagnet. Usually, any problems show up right after installation. Ninety-five percent of the time, the problem is either an improperly mounted armature or improper voltage input. Follow the manufacturer's instructions for mounting the armature, and use the hardware supplied. Remember, in almost all cases, the armature should be free to float. When the armature is rigid, it will not bond properly to the magnet, as it is trying to overcome all the unevenness of the door surface.

Checking the magnetism by placing a screwdriver blade on the face of the magnet will only indicate if the magnetic field exists. You will be able to pull the screwdriver off. To have a true holding force, the mass of the armature must be used to complete the magnetic bond.

Since all magnets need DC voltage, make sure that if you have low-voltage AC power, there is a rectifier between it and the magnet. Also, be sure that the input voltage is the value required by the magnet.

The following are some of the symptoms that the electromagnet may exhibit and their probable causes:

No holding force: Check the input power at the magnet. Make sure that it is DC voltage if the magnet does not have a rectifier option or is not marked for AC operation. If the correct voltage is present, the magnet could be defective, which is rare. If there is no voltage at the magnet, check the line power, electrical connections, and hookup of access control devices.

Weak holding force: Check the armature mounting; it should allow for slight movement of the armature. Check for lower than rated voltage, which could be caused by low line power, long wire runs over too small a wire gauge, or an improper power supply. If AC power is applied to a DC-only magnet, a slight humming or vibration may be present. Dirt or some other interference between mating faces will also reduce the holding force.

Works intermittently: Check for loose wire connections. Also check for proper operation of whatever access control devices are controlling the magnet.

ELECTROMECHANICAL LOCKS

I use the term *electromechanical locks* to cover the general range of electrified bored and mortise builders' hardware locks (see Figures 3–12 and 3–13). Included in this category are several other specialty and detention locking devices that are similar in nature. All of these devices are combinations of a mechanical lock and an electric solenoid that controls either the knob or lever or the latchbolt.

I will not detail the functions and mechanisms of these locks, as most of you should be familiar with this type of builders' hardware. For those who are not knowledgeable in this area, I recommend that you study manufacturers' literature or take a course in builders' hardware. This will aid you in the initial selection of these types of locks.

Figure 3–12.   Electrified bored lock. (Courtesy of Sargent)

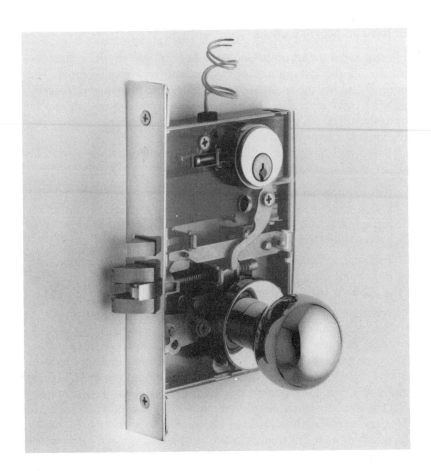

Figure 3–13. Electrified mortise lock. (Courtesy of Schlage Lock Co.)

These devices are electrified to provide convenience, higher security, and better life safety features. A solenoid is added to the mechanism that controls a linkage that enables or disables either the knob or
the latchbolt. As in the electric locks discussed earlier, the solenoid is
operated by a low-voltage power source and is controlled either lo-
cally or remotely by access control devices.

Many of the locks covered in this section are UL-listed for labeled
doors. Many also conform to ASA and ANSI standards and require
standard preparation for door and frame.

Bored and Mortise Locks

Electric locking and unlocking of bored and mortise locks involves controlling the locking hub of the mechanism with a solenoid. This normally allows the secure-side knob or lever to be locked electrically. Mortise locks may also be selected with electric locking features on both sides. The electric unlocking operation normally does not retract the latch but frees the knob or lever for use.

Bored and mortise locks are available in both fail-safe and fail-secure modes, as follows:

Fail-safe, power normally on: The latchbolt is retracted by both knobs, except if the outside knob is locked electrically. The key retracts the latchbolt from the outside. The lock unlocks when power is off. The inside knob is always free.

Fail-secure, power normally off: The key retracts the latchbolt from the outside. The outside knob is always locked unless electric power is applied. The inside knob is always free.

Note: Some mortise locks are available in which both knobs are controlled electrically.

Most of these locks do not offer optional monitoring switches. They are generally available in 12- or 24-volt, AC or DC, and some offer 115VAC operation. Normally, current ratings run from 1.0 amp and under, but some heavy-duty mortise locks draw up to 8 amps.

One company provides the unique service of modifying standard builders' hardware locks to incorporate electric operation. All manufacturer's mortise and unit locks and mortise and rim panic devices are modified with a solenoid to lock and unlock the lever, knob, or thumbpiece. Monitoring switches are also offered as part of the modification. Although I noted earlier that attempting to electrify a mechanical lock is not a good idea, in this case all modifications are expertly engineered by experienced personnel.

Some general uses for electric bored and mortise locks are stairwell and security doors, commercial buildings, institutions, apartments, banks, interlocks, and fire safety applications.

Mortise Locks for Exit Devices

Several manufacturers offer solenoid-operated mortise locks for exit devices. This combination offers the safety features of the exit device with the added security of electrical control. The lock controls the locking of the outside thumbpiece or knob of the exit device. When it is unlocked, the door remains latched, preserving the fire rating of the door. This is particularly useful where codes permit locking but require unlocking during a fire emergency.

These locks are available in both fail-safe and fail-secure modes, as follows:

Fail-safe, power normally on: The solenoid locks the outside trim. The thumbpiece, knob, or lever is then free-acting and disengaged. The key retracts the latchbolt at all times.

Fail-secure, power normally off: When energized, the solenoid unlocks the outside trim. The thumbpiece, knob, or lever can then retract the latchbolt. The key retracts the latchbolt at all times.

Note: Some fire codes require fail-safe operation for stairwell doors. High-security facilities, such as high-rise office buildings, may require fail-secure operation.

These locks are available in 12- or 24-volt, AC or DC. Current ratings can run quite high, some ranging from 4 to 8 amps.

Strike Actuators

Another device for electrically controlling mortise locks is a solenoid-operated actuator in the strike plate of a mortise lock with an auxiliary latch (see Figure 3–14). One manufacturer offers it as a stock item along with their mortise lockset. Another manufacturer offers a custom unit that they will mate with any standard mortise lock sent to them for modification. An advantage of this type of unit is that it keeps the electrical wiring in the frame. It fits into ANSI standard strike preparations and requires no special door or frame preparation.

Locking of the knob or lever is accomplished by a plunger in the strike plate assembly. The plunger is extended or retracted by the solenoid, which is also in the strike assembly. The plunger is positioned over the auxiliary latch of the mortise lock in the door. By depressing or releasing the auxiliary latch, it controls the locking hub in the mortise lock. The actuator is available in both fail-safe and fail-secure modes as follows:

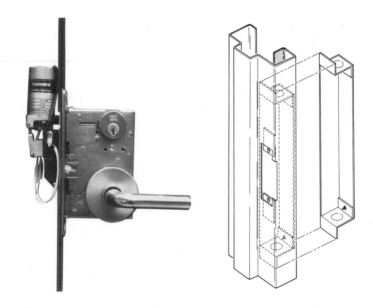

Figure 3–14. Custom strike actuator and modified mortise lockset (left) with recommended mortar guard (back box, right). (Courtesy of Architectural Control Systems, Inc.)

Fail-safe, power normally on: When the solenoid is energized, the plunger extends, depressing the auxiliary latch. The mortise lock hub is then locked until power is interrupted.

Fail-secure, power normally off: The plunger is extended, depressing the auxiliary latch. When power is applied, the solenoid retracts the plunger, releasing the auxiliary latch. The locking hub is then unlocked until power is interrupted.

These devices are generally available in 12- or 24-volt, AC or DC, and some units are available in 115VAC. Current ratings usually run 1.5 amps and under.

A similar frame-mounted unit offers much the same features, except that it can deadlock the mortise lock without requiring an auxiliary deadlocking cam linkage. It is available with a mortise lockset, or any major manufacturer's mortise lockset can be modified to work with it. Latch position and door secure sensors are available options on this unit.

Another version of this concept offers a double locking system, primarily used for stairtower safety and security. To my knowledge, it is offered by only one manufacturer and is recognized in the industry by its trade name, HiTower. The electric lock portion of this system mounts in the frame. It includes an electrically operated bolt and a strike for the mortise lock latch. It is available in both fail-safe and fail-secure modes. The standard operating voltage is 115VAC, but it is also available in 24VAC or 24VDC. Lock status and door position monitoring options are also available.

The mortise lock portion of the system mounts in the door. It is a heavy-duty lock incorporating a strike for the electric bolt. This system allows remote electric locking and unlocking without unlatching the mortise lock. This keeps the door latched until it is opened by the key on the secure side or by the knob or lever on the free side.

The system meets the specifications of basic fire codes, and it is popular for high-rise building stairtower doors. The system is also applicable in numerous other areas of schools, hospitals, correctional facilities, and government and commercial buildings.

Detention and High-Security Locks

Although detention hardware would require a separate study entirely, I will briefly mention some of these locking devices because of their use in a variety of other areas. These types of locks are all mortise-style and offer the same functions as the mortise locks already discussed. Their construction is somewhat different, however, because they are all built for heavy-duty use. All offer monitoring options and other high-security features not found on standard hardware.

It should also be noted that these locks are rated for higher operating voltages, and some draw considerable current. In some cases, two current ratings, inrush and seated, are listed. The inrush current is a short-duration, high-current draw to initiate the action of the mechanism. Once activated, the current required to hold (or seat) the mechanism in its changed state drops off to a lower requirement. The power supply must be able to supply the highest current requirement, regardless of its short duration.

Although these locks are primarily designed for detention and prison environments, they are also used in commercial and industrial buildings where high security is required.

OTHER ELECTRONIC DEVICES

Several other electronic devices, though not strictly electric locks, provide electric control of doors.

Electronic Exit Devices

Exit devices are a required hardware item in almost every building. They provide for both the safety and the security of an opening, preventing unauthorized entry while allowing safe egress at all times.

Electronic exit devices provide greater control over the opening and allow interfacing with other electronic equipment. The market tends to be dominated by a single manufacturer, which offers a solenoid-operated lock that either controls the latchbolt of a device or controls the locking of the operating trim (see Figure 3–15A). The solenoids draw a heavy inrush current. A typical rating is 24VDC, 16 amp inrush, 0.3 amp holding. The inrush current duration is about a quarter of a second.

There are two methods of controlling the electric locking and unlocking of the exit device. With the first method, the solenoid retracts the latch and holds it retracted until power to the solenoid is interrupted. The device is "dogged" electrically, and the door becomes a push-pull operation. Doors in office buildings, schools, or department stores can be controlled from a central point and kept dogged during working hours. All doors can be relatched simultaneously at closing time or during a fire emergency by a central fire panel tie-in.

The other method controls the operating trim, allowing the device to remain latched. The exterior knob, lever, or thumbpiece is locked or unlocked electrically to control entry. This type of locking is available in either fail-safe or fail-secure modes. The fail-safe mode would be used on labeled stairwell openings, where doors must be available for reentry from the stair side during a fire emergency.

Monitoring switches are also available for electronic exit devices. The latchbolt position is the function most often monitored to indicate whether the latchbolt is extended and a secure condition exists. Oper-

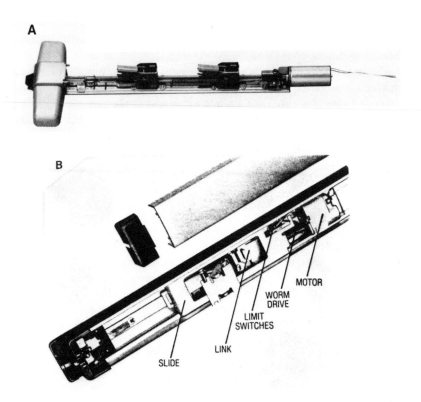

Figure 3–15. (A) Exit device with electric solenoid. (Courtesy of Von Duprin) (B) Exit device with electric motor. (Courtesy of Adams Rite Mfg. Co.)

ating trim may also be monitored to indicate whether the opening is being used for egress or entry. If the monitoring switches are being used to activate an alarm signal, a built-in alarm shunt key switch option is also offered.

Whenever electric locking or monitoring is used, provisions must be made for carrying the power or monitor signal from the door to the frame. Electric hinges and pivots are available for this purpose (see Chapter 6). Where high current is being carried, a heavy-duty power transfer set is available for installations using butt hinges. Its heavy conductors, both 18AWG, make it ideal for handling heavy inrush currents. It is rated for 24VDC, 10-amp service and will carry 20-amp maximum surges. When the door is closed, the device is fully concealed and tamper-resistant.

Several other manufacturers offer electric devices, but with limited features and variety. One offers a solenoid-operated device that draws only 0.3 amp because of a unique latch and strike mechanism. The solenoid controls the latch mechanism only. This device is offered with an electric alarm option that has a key shunt override.

Another manufacturer offers a line of mechanical devices with a motor control option (see Figure 3–15B). A small 24VDC motor is built into the pushbar. The motor, which controls the latching device, draws only 0.3 amp and offers very high torque to overcome side loads. The trade-off is that it does not react as fast as a solenoid. Unlatching times are listed as one second for rim devices, two seconds for mortise devices, and four seconds for vertical rod devices.

Electronic exit devices provide remote locking control, which is useful where it is desirable to have free-swinging doors during certain hours. They also allow interfacing with automatic door operators. If the device is fire-rated it may also be used on labeled openings when it is under the control of an approved automatic fire alarm system. It is the fire alarm system that releases the fail-safe solenoid to ensure latching during an emergency.

Exit Device Latch Releases

Some fire-rated openings are equipped with automatic door operators and vertical rod exit devices. During automatic operation, the top and bottom exit device latches remain retracted, allowing the door to open and close freely. During a fire emergency, the door must be closed and latched.

The latch release device is an electromagnetic unit that allows the exit device latch tripper to remain free, keeping the latchbolts retracted during normal use. In an emergency, the latch release, which is tied into the fire alarm system, is deenergized. A signal switch instantly deactivates the door operator. A spring-loaded trigger is simultaneously released and automatically activates the latch tripper when the door closes. The door is then latched and subject to manual operation only. When it is determined that the emergency condition is over, the exit device and latch release are manually reset.

The unit operates by a 24-volt AC or DC (.08 amp) fail-safe electromagnet. It is also available for 12-volt AC or DC (.18 amp) operation.

Door Closers/Holders

Other popular electronic door control devices are the door holder and the combination door closer/holder. They are standard builders' hardware items offered by several manufacturers. These devices are commonly used on smoke- or fire-rated openings where the door is normally held in an open position. During a smoke or fire alarm, the devices release the doors. Doors equipped with combination closer/ holders will release and close automatically. Doors equipped with holders must also have mechanical closers.

These units are generally available in 120VAC, 12-volt AC or DC, and 24-volt AC or DC. There are several available for 240VAC operation. All these units draw very little current, and all are UL-listed.

The combination closer/holder units generally require 15 to 20 pounds force to manually close the door. Many models are offered with built-in smoke detectors and alarm signal output contacts (see Figure 3–16). Most lock into the alarm condition and provide a manual reset button. A variety of models are available for different door and frame conditions.

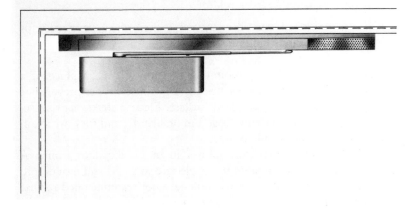

Figure 3–16. Combination holder/closer with built-in smoke detector. (Courtesy of LCN Closers)

Electromagnetic door holders generally run from 20 to 40 pounds holding force. They are available in several variations of wall and floor mounts. Popular applications include smoke and fire barrier doors, horizontal exit doors, patient room doors, and stairway doors (where applicable).

REVIEW

Electric locks fall into four basic categories:

1. Electric strikes
2. Electric deadbolts
3. Electromagnets
4. Electromechanical locks

All of these devices operate on the principle of electromagnetism.

All electric locking devices operate at a specific voltage at which they draw a specific current. Most operate on low-voltage AC or DC. The choice between AC and DC is generally one of convenience, unless the type of lock selected must be operated from one specific current.

The two most common operating modes are as follows:

Fail-secure: unlocked when energized, locked when deenergized; fails into secure (locked) mode.

Fail-safe: unlocked when deenergized, locked when energized; fails into safe (unlocked) mode.

Electric strikes generally mount in the door frame in place of a conventional lock strike. An electrically controlled keeper prevents or allows the latching of a standard lockset. Electric strikes can be selected to operate with an audible sound or silently, and they are available either fail-safe or fail-secure.

Electric deadbolts generally mount in or on the door frame. A spring-loaded bolt is activated by an electric solenoid and moves into or out of a mating strike. Electric bolts are not recommended for use on doors with panic hardware. They are available either fail-safe or fail-secure.

Electromagnets normally mount on the door frame. They consist of two parts: the magnet and the mating armature plate, which mounts on the door. They have no moving mechanisms and are available only as fail-safe units.

Electromechanical locks include a wide range of electrified bored and mortise locksets. There are also specialty locks and high-security locks with similar operating mechanisms. They are all combinations of a mechanical lock operated by an electric solenoid and, sometimes, a motor. They are available either fail-safe or fail-secure.

4

The Power Source

The power source for a locking device must be designed or selected to provide the correct amount of current, at a specific voltage, that is needed to operate the locking device and any other electric load within the system.

Throughout this chapter, we will be discussing the use of low-voltage power for electric locking devices. I have always regarded the use of low voltage at a door as primarily a life safety feature. As evident in the National Electrical Code, any electrical equipment that operates at 50 volts or more has much more stringent standards regarding location, protection, conduit, and so on.

For most manufacturers, low voltage is considered standard for powering electric locking devices and associated equipment, such as monitoring devices. In many cases, low-voltage DC is specified to allow the use of uninterruptible standby power through standby battery power systems. In addition, the popularity of computer-based control circuitry has made low-voltage equipment more desirable for interfacing in systems design.

Power sources for electric locking systems range from simple transformers to complex packages with built-in logic circuitry. Some of the power sources we will be studying are:

1. Step-down transformers
2. AC power supplies

3. DC power supplies
4. Regulated DC power supplies
5. Special output power supplies
6. Uninterruptible power supplies (DC units with rechargeable standby batteries)
7. Power controllers with logic circuitry

To simplify the lesson plan, I like to divide power sources into three distinct levels. These levels are progressive in their degree of complexity, the simplest being the basic *transformer*. The next step up from a transformer is the *power supply*, followed by the *power controller*. It should be noted that the use of the simplest unit, the transformer, usually requires the most knowledge by the user. The more complex units normally have built-in features that eliminate the need for circuit design. They can be selected to provide the circuit requirements for a specific system and require little more work than hookup of each system component to it.

INTRODUCTION TO ELECTRIC POWER

As I noted earlier, this book is intended to be simple enough to help hardware people engage in electrical hardware work. It is not intended to provide instruction in electrical engineering. The information presented in this chapter is boiled down to provide basic information essential only to the subject of the book.

Electricity originates in generating plants and is produced at many thousands of volts. It is usually necessary to transmit thousands of kilowatts of power over great distances. The cost of wire large enough to transmit the power at 120 or even 240 volts would be prohibitive. High voltages can be transmitted great distances over relatively small wire and with less voltage loss, but these high voltages are too dangerous to be used with ordinary equipment.

There must be a convenient way to change from one voltage to another as needed. For everyday needs, there is no simple or efficient way of doing this with direct current (DC); however, there is a simple and efficient means of doing it with alternating current (AC). The transformer is used to change from one AC voltage to another.

Power plants produce various voltages; 13,800 volts is typical, as shown in Figure 4–1. Transformers can be used to step up the gener-

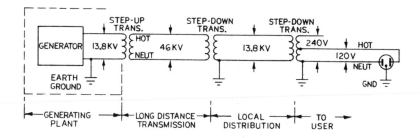

Figure 4–1. Power transmission.

ated voltage to a much higher voltage for transmission over long distances. At various substations, the transmission voltages are stepped down for distribution. At other points, they may again be reduced to even lower distribution voltages.

It is at the generating plant that the difference between a "hot" and a "neutral" wire is determined. The neutral wire is physically connected to the earth to provide earth ground potential. Wiring in buildings also provides a third wire, which is also connected to earth ground.

For safety reasons, building wiring is color-coded. The hot wire is black, the white wire is neutral, and the green wire is ground. If you were to touch the black and white wires simultaneously, you would complete a circuit and receive a dangerous shock. Touching the black wire while you are in good contact with earth ground can produce the same results (see Figure 4–2). Touching the white (neutral) wire will not cause a shock, as it is already at earth ground and would not complete a circuit. As you may already know, standing on a nonconductive material, such as a heavy rubber mat, can save you from a severe electrical shock. The nonconductive material prevents completion of the circuit and the flow of current through your body.

The additional wire, green to ground, is to provide safety when using appliances. For example, in an electric drill, the black and white wires are connected directly to the motor of the drill so that it will operate. Suppose that, because of a defect, the hot wire inside the drill touches the drill housing. If you were to touch the housing while some other part of your body was in good contact with an earth ground, you would receive a shock. However, the third (green) wire is attached to the housing, connecting it to earth ground. The hot wire touching

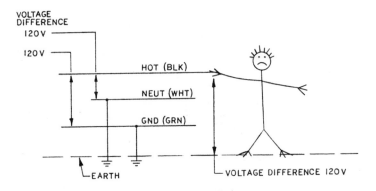

Figure 4–2. High-voltage electrical shock.

the housing would cause an immediate short circuit and blow a fuse. The current flow in the short circuit would follow the path of least resistance, which would be from hot wire to housing to green wire to ground. This would save you from becoming part of the circuit and receiving a shock (see Figure 4–3).

I have purposely provided detailed discussion and diagrams for this part of the lesson to impress upon you that you should never cut off the ground pin on the plug of your electric tools!

Getting back to the transmission of electricity, it should be noted that transformers operate only on alternating current. There are many advantages to long-distance transmission of direct current, but the procedures involved are feasible only for very large amounts of power

Figure 4–3. Grounding pin shock protection.

transmitted from a single point to another distant single point. Later in this chapter, we will cover the conversion of AC power to DC power.

TRANSFORMERS

As mentioned earlier, transformers change one AC voltage to another AC voltage. Transformers are available in a great variety of styles for a great variety of purposes. In this text, we will concern ourselves only with the simple step-down transformer.

The most common primary source of power you will be confronted with will be 120VAC, 50/60Hz (cycles per second). Regardless of the actual power supplied to a building, in most cases you will be provided with 120VAC in the vicinity of the work being done. You may still hear references to 110- and 220-volt current, which long ago were the usual voltages, but 120 and 240 are the nominal voltages in use today, and the National Electrical Code requires that load calculations be based on them. Generally, a variation of plus or minus 15 percent in the 120 line voltage will not adversely affect electronic security devices. If you should find a greater variation than 102 to 138 volts at the source, it should be reported to an electrician.

The transformer is the device that joins AC power from the source to the load. The power source is connected to the primary winding and the load to the secondary winding. During the process, certain changes take place that are related to the construction of the transformer.

The job of the step-down transformer is to reduce the 120VAC power source to a lower AC voltage, as required by the load. The most common lower AC voltage is 24V, but you will also find use for a range of voltages, as noted in Chapter 3.

The transformer has no moving parts. It consists of two coils of wire or windings on a core made of thin laminations of silicon iron, as shown in Figure 4–4. The two windings and the core are electrically insulated from one another.

The transformer operates on a principle known as *electromagnetic induction*. Applying 120VAC across the primary or input side winding causes current to flow in the primary coil. The primary current alternates from positive to negative sixty times a second. This sets up a changing magnetic field in the iron core, known as *flux*. This field is constantly changing—expanding, collapsing, expanding, collapsing, and so on—with each change in the alternating current. The changing

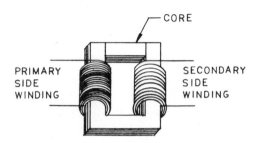

Figure 4–4.   Basic construction of a step-down transformer.

flux induces voltage in any winding it surrounds; the greater the number of turns in the winding, the greater the induced voltage. At this point, it is easy to see why transformers do not operate on direct current. Direct current sets up a steady magnetic field and cannot induce voltage in the windings.

The changing magnetic field carried by the core cuts the windings of the secondary coil, inducing a voltage in it. When a load is connected across the secondary or output side, current flows in the load. If the primary and secondary coils had the same number of turns, the input and output voltages would also be the same. This type of transformer is called an *isolation transformer*. As with all transformers it isolates, or keeps separate, the input voltage side from the output voltage side. Since we are interested in a step-down transformer, we want to reduce the voltage of the output side.

The voltage in the secondary side is lowered by reducing the number of turns in its winding in proportion to the number of turns in the primary side winding. During all this transforming from one voltage to another, there are power losses that do not permit 100-percent efficiency in transfer of power from source to load. Although these losses are of no concern to us, one of the conditions causing some power loss will be noticed as heat. For this reason, a warm transformer, when under load, is a normal condition.

Before discussing how to select a transformer, I will cover one more technical point that will be of interest to us later when we cover DC power supplies.

As already mentioned, it is the alternating of the current from positive to negative that creates the magnetic field. This change of

polarity or cycle can be measured by an oscilloscope. On the oscilloscope, one complete change in polarity or cycle would look like the
diagram in Figure 4–5. The height of the *sine wave*, as it is called,
would equal the peak voltage (V). We are interested in the rated or
average voltage, which is 0.707 of the peak voltage. In Figure 4–5, the
curve ranges between 0 and 170 volts, giving us a 120V average. The
length of the cycle is measured in time (*t*). In our example, the length
of *t* would be one-sixtieth of a second.

What we have shown is 120VAC at 60 cycles per second, properly
called 60Hz. When we step the 120VAC down to a lower voltage, the
cycles per second—60Hz—remain the same. In the United States,
Canada, and most of Mexico, standard commercial current is 60Hz.
In other countries, most installations are 50Hz, with a trend toward
60Hz.

The reason I have explained the alternating cycles of voltage in such
detail is to give you a better understanding of what causes an electric
strike to buzz or chatter, as described in Chapter 3. If you have ever
put your finger in a 120VAC light socket, you have some idea of this
by the buzzing sensation you felt!

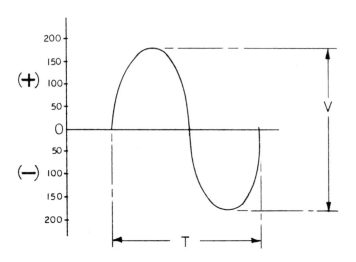

Figure 4–5. Diagram of one cycle of AC voltage.

SELECTING A TRANSFORMER

Once you understand how a transformer works, the actual selection of a transformer for a particular system is relatively simple. The first thing you must determine is the power requirements of the load. After selecting the locking device for the system, you must determine two factors: its operating voltage and how much current it draws. As explained in Chapter 3, this information is either marked on the unit itself or contained in the manufacturer's literature. Remember, if the current or power requirements are expressed in watts, change watts to amps by the formula:

$$\frac{\text{watts}}{\text{operating voltage}} = \text{amps}$$

Note, also, that if a lock is marked, for example, 24VAC/DC, it will operate on *either* 24VAC or 24VDC. A transformer is fully acceptable for such a device.

I am often asked, "What operating voltage should I choose?" This really isn't very important, as you are always starting with 120VAC and converting it to a lower voltage. The two most popular voltages are 12 and 24 volts, with 24V the most popular; 24V units usually draw less current than 12V units. It is just as easy to obtain 12V transformers, however, and this voltage is used extensively in the alarm industry.

When selecting the locking device, you may want to use the same low voltage as other items in supporting systems on the job, just for consistency. Other items may include separate alarm systems or access control devices with their own power systems. Another selection factor may be simply the availability of the unit from the manufacturer or distributor.

Once the lock's operating or input voltage and current requirements are determined, you can select the transformer in much the same way you select a lock. Read the manufacturers' literature to find a step-down transformer that matches your input and output voltage needs. In the literature, the input voltage may be listed under "primary volts" and the output voltage under "secondary volts." The current capacity should also be listed under "secondary amps." Often, the power capacity will be listed as VA, or volt/amps. As explained in Chapter 2, volt/amps can be converted to amps by the formula:

$$\frac{\text{volt/amps (VA)}}{\text{rated output voltage}} = \text{capacity in amps}$$

Like locking devices, the transformer should be well marked with its input and output specifications. A transformer may be listed or marked with a slightly higher than needed output voltage. For example, when you are looking for a 24VAC output you may find a 25.2VAC output listed. This rating was necessary in vacuum tube circuits in older-model radios. It is a practical rating to use when the output voltage is to be rectified to direct current for DC-operated locks. As will be shown later in this chapter, there is a small voltage loss through a rectifier, and the higher rating will allow for this loss. A transformer at this rating is also perfectly acceptable to use with a 24VAC locking device. It is recommended that you select an output amperage higher than you actually need. A 25 to 50 percent higher amperage rating will not affect the locking device and allows you the comfort of knowing that you have sufficient power for the job. Skimping on the capacity of the transformer to save money can cause problems later with a poorly operating locking device.

If the transformer is to power more than one lock, the amperages for all locks must be totaled before you can select the correct transformer. Any other loads—such as monitoring lights—must also be added to this total.

Transformers with a *center tap* (CT) are very common. You may find a transformer with a secondary rated at 24 CT. This means that you have a choice of using the two outside wires for 24VAC output or using either one of the outside wires and the center wire for a 12VAC output. Whichever wire is not used can be insulated and coiled up with electrical tape and left on the transformer. It also can be cut off at the winding, but it would no longer be available if needed.

If a transformer is center-tapped and you use the center wire, you will always get half the rated output voltage but the same capacity in amperage. There are transformers with multiple taps on both the primary and secondary sides, but you will probably never need these.

Transformers come in all shapes and sizes; the types shown in Figures 4–6 and 4–7 are the ones you will work with most often. The transformer in Figure 4–6 has terminals coming out of it and provides bolt-down mounting tabs. It would be electrically connected in the system using crimp-on terminals on the lead wires. By far the easiest to

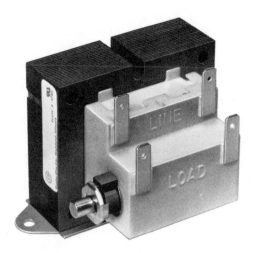

Figure 4–6.   Bolt-down transformer with quick-connect terminals. (Courtesy of Basler Electric)

Figure 4–7.   Plug-in transformer with screw-type output terminals. (Courtesy of Basler Electric)

use is the plug-in transformer shown in Figure 4–7. It simply plugs into an electrical outlet, usually located out of plain sight, and connections to it are made by screw terminals. Figure 4–8 illustrates the wiring of a simple system using a plug-in transformer.

The question of code conformance frequently arises regarding the use of any electrical security device. The rules governing the use of transformers are covered in National Electrical Code (NEC) Article 450. The requirements for the types of transformers we will be studying are defined in UL 506 and CSA (Canadian Standards Association) C22.2, No. 66.

Understanding these codes would require some heavy reading, but in most cases you will be safe if you follow a simple rule: Always select a UL-listed or UL-recognized Class II transformer. This type of transformer should comply with all the requirements of local codes. Check the local codes for the type of transformer construction allowed. Some areas do not allow plug-in transformers and require the use of hard-wired transformers. In these cases, you should select a UL Class II transformer with leads or "pigtails" on both the primary and the secondary sides. At any rate, the use of UL Class II transformers may eliminate disputes with local electrical inspectors over possible code violations.

What a Class II transformer provides is built-in overcurrent protection. National Electrical Code Article 450 covers the installation of all

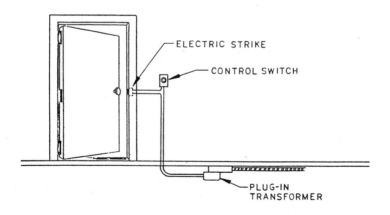

Figure 4–8. Diagram of a simple electric locking system.

transformers. It thoroughly details how to provide overcurrent protection for all types of transformers. Many transformers available in manufacturers' catalogs do not provide built-in overcurrent protection. The protection must be added, in compliance with these regulations, to the system or product in which the transformer is being used. Such transformers are commonly purchased by manufacturers that build them into their own product, which, in turn, may be UL-tested and labeled as a separate unit.

Different types of overcurrent protection are built into Class II transformers. Normally, you won't have to be concerned with the details of the protection the unit provides, but the following are several types of overcurrent protection available in Class II transformers:

1. One-shot thermal fuse that opens when temperature limit is exceeded
2. One-shot current fuse that opens when secondary is shorted and one-shot thermal fuse that opens when temperature limit is exceeded
3. Automatic resetting thermobreaker
4. Energy-limiting design such that after the primary is energized and the secondary is shorted, the secondary is limited, in one minute, to 8 amps (the secondary may be shorted for very short periods without damage)

The only other point that may need consideration is the location of the transformer. National Electrical Code Article 450.2 states that the transformer must be readily accessible for inspection and maintenance. There are several exceptions to this rule, and it appears that the type of low-voltage, low-current transformer you would be using would fall under these exceptions. I say "appears" because it is always advisable to check local codes.

TROUBLESHOOTING TRANSFORMERS

Because they have no moving parts and are completely static solid state devices, transformers have long and trouble-free lives under normal operating conditions. They are normally well tested by the manufacturer, and defective devices are rare.

Three characteristics of the transformer that are sometimes noticeable are usually no cause for alarm:

1. *Heat:* It is typical for a transformer operating under normal conditions to be warm to the touch. If a transformer feels hot, it could be overloaded, and its output rating should be checked to be sure it is high enough to handle the load rating. A problem in the operation of the load could also cause this condition, and the device being powered should be checked for faulty operation or wiring. Overheating due to excessive operating temperature will result in deterioration of the insulation and eventual failure of the transformer coils. A sudden high overload can be detected by an obvious and offensive odor, and the power should be cut immediately. One cause of a rapid overload condition would be if the transformer were inadvertently wired in reverse. Also note that in no case should a transformer be operated at a higher voltage than its nameplate rating.

2. *Audible noise:* Some transformers may emit a humming sound. This could be caused by a poorly constructed transformer or one in which the transformer laminations have become slightly loosened. A humming noise may also be the result of a transformer not being securely mounted. If the sound is barely audible or is not offensive to the end user, the transformer need not be replaced, as it will most likely operate efficiently for its full rated life span.

3. *Electrical noise:* This not so noticeable characteristic is caused by stray magnetic flux leaking from the core and windings and interacting with nearby wiring and electronic components. The "noise" referred to here is not something you can hear; rather, it is an interference with nearby signal-carrying conductors or susceptible components. The best prevention is to keep the power supply components away from any low-signal level circuitry or devices. You may never be confronted with this problem, but I will give you a general example of such a situation: If an unshielded cable from a solid state access control device, such as a card reader, is run in the vicinity of the transformer or power supply, the electrical noise could cause some sort of feedback or interference through the wiring, thus causing improper operation of the solid state device.

When a transformer is suspected of being faulty, there is really only one quick test you need to perform. Once again, you will need to use a multimeter or voltmeter, as discussed in Chapter 9. With the transformer primary hooked up and the load disconnected from the secondary, check the voltage output across the secondary leads. It should read within a couple of volts of its rated output—normally, several volts higher. It would be best to check the primary source also, which should read close to 120VAC. This, too, may vary—anywhere from 102VAC to 138VAC; if it is high or low, the secondary reading will also be slightly higher or lower than its rating.

If the secondary voltage is checked with the load hooked up, the reading will drop by one or two volts from the no-load reading and should read close to its rated voltage. In any case, if a transformer is bad, it will most likely show a zero voltage reading. Always be sure that you have the meter on the correct setting and are reading the correct scale on needle-type meters.

REVIEW OF TRANSFORMERS

Alternating current (AC) reverses its voltage polarity and current flow at a definite rate. This rate is called cycles per second (cps) or Hertz (Hz). AC is created by power generators and is stepped down by transformers to working voltages. The most common AC commercial voltage is 120VAC, 60Hz. The most common lower AC voltage is 24VAC, 60Hz. Be extremely careful when working with power in excess of 50 volts.

A transformer consists of two or more windings on a core. When an AC source is applied across the primary winding, a voltage is induced in the secondary winding. If a load is connected to the secondary, current also flows in that winding.

The step-down transformer changes a high AC input voltage to a lower, safer AC output voltage. It therefore is a device that couples AC power from a source connected to the primary to a load connected to the secondary.

A transformer is rated in nominal volts AC and the maximum current it can supply. The AC output of the transformer must match the AC voltage required by the load.

The transformer output current (amperes) should be selected to provide 25 to 50 percent more current than is required by the load in the system. It does not matter how high the rated output current is, because the load will use only the amount of current for which it is rated.

A transformer with a center tap (CT) allows you the choice of selecting either the full rated output voltage (i.e., 24VAC) or half the rating (i.e., 12VAC).

Transformers are available in many different hookup configurations, including leads, plug-ins, screw terminals, and so on. The safest approach is to select UL Class II transformers. They are designed with built-in overcurrent protection. Consult national and local electrical codes for allowable types of transformers, wiring, location, and so forth.

Moderate heating and humming does not indicate a faulty transformer. The easiest way to determine a faulty transformer is to check the output voltage with a voltmeter. It should read slightly higher than the rating (without a load).

Your increasing knowledge will guide you in selecting the proper transformer. When questions arise, consult the distributor or manufacturer of the device you are powering for help in selecting the correct power supply. Electrical supply houses can be helpful, as they normally carry the most popular transformers and they should be familiar with local code requirements.

Example of Transformer Selection

Problem
Select a transformer rated to operate two fail-safe electric locks and two "lock on" indicator lights in a single system. The locks are rated for 6 watts at 24VAC, and the lights are rated 28V, .04A.

Solution
Since both the locks and the lights will be energized at the same time, the total current draw must be determined. Convert watts to amps as follows:

$$\frac{6 \text{ watts}}{24 \text{ volts}} = .25 \text{ amps}$$

Total all current draws in system:

$$.25 + .25 + .04 + .04 = .58A$$

Allowing a 50 percent margin (.58 × 1.5 = .87 amps), a transformer rated 24VAC, 1 amp (or higher) output would be acceptable.

Since many transformers are rated in volt/amps (VA), .87 amps can be converted to VA: 24V (rated output) × .87 = 20.9VA. Thus, a transformer rated 20VA (or higher) would be acceptable.

POWER SUPPLIES

As we have seen, the transformer simply provides low-voltage AC to devices rated to operate from that type of power. I refer to the next higher level in power sources as a *power supply,* although that very general term is used in the industry to cover a great variety of power units available on the market.

For purposes of our discussion, the power supply commonly consists of the following items:

1. The primary side *fuse,* rated to match the supply, protects against excessive current draw in the primary, which could be caused by overloading or dead-shorting the supply output.
2. The *grounding screw,* normally provided, is used to connect the third, or ground, wire of the AC input cable to create a path from the power supply to earth ground.
3. The *transformer* reduces the 120VAC line power to a lower AC voltage. It also provides electrical isolation between the primary and secondary windings.
4. The *rectifier bridge* (DC units only) changes low-voltage AC to low-voltage DC.
5. The *terminal board* is usually a screw-type terminal block for hookup of external components.

All of these items are normally mounted in some type of electrical box—typically, a steel enclosure with a hinged or removable cover. Conduit knockouts around the sides provide for wiring ingress/egress.

The benefits of using this type of unit are the ease of making the system connections and the convenience of the electrical box for mounting the entire package. Having a common tie-point for the external component hookups greatly facilitates troubleshooting.

The method of selection is much the same as that for selecting a transformer. Always be sure that the output rating of the power supply is compatible with the operating rating of the load.

AC POWER SUPPLIES

The first question that usually arises is why you should spend extra money on an AC power supply when a UL Class II transformer will do. First, as mentioned earlier, it provides a convenient way to make system electrical connections. Like the DC unit shown later (in Figure 4–11), the AC unit provides screw terminals for tie-in of the load and control switch. The value of your time spent hand-wiring components together in a system would probably exceed the few extra dollars spent on the power supply. In terms of the actual electrical hookup, the use of this type of terminal board can provide much more reliable connections.

A second benefit is the single-point location of the electrical connections. The system wire runs can be prewired and brought to a common location, where the power supply will act as a junction box. Most troubleshooting of a system can normally be done at this single location.

Another point to consider is the needed capacity of the power supply. Typically, plug-in transformers are limited in available current ratings. In systems where high current is required, a much larger transformer may be required; a power supply can provide the higher current capacity. If you were to use only a transformer, it would be advisable to provide fuse protection in the circuit, whereas replaceable primary side fusing is usually incorporated in the power supply.

The following formula can be used for calculating a primary side fuse size, but it is part of a complex procedure for those who desire to piece together their own power supplies. I highly recommend that you purchase an applicable power supply and leave design problems to the electrical engineers. The formula is as follows:

Total current draw on secondary side (total all loads	Step-down ratio (transformer secondary voltage divided by primary voltage)	Current draw on primary side	Safety factor	Primary side fuse size
	$\times$	=	$\times$	=

$$10A \times \frac{24}{120} \qquad = 2A \qquad \times 2 \qquad = 4A$$

The selection process for an AC power supply is pretty much identical to the process for selecting a transformer. Although transformers are available from many sources, your best sources of power supplies are probably the electric locking device manufacturers or their distributors.

DC POWER SUPPLIES

Until now, we have studied only AC power requirements. Now we will look at the differences between AC and DC power. The polarity of direct current does not change in cycles, as alternating current does (see Figure 4–5). As discussed in Chapter 3, all electromagnetic devices must be operated by DC power. The exception is an AC-operated electric strike where a buzzing sound is desirable. If the same strike were powered by DC, it would operate more efficiently and would no longer buzz. This is because DC flows directly from negative (−) to positive (+) in one continuous cycle.

The simplest source of DC power is the battery. The battery, however, is severely limited in the amount and life span of the power it can deliver. For these reasons, we must find a more acceptable source of DC power—that is, conversion of our basic AC power into DC power. Although DC cannot be converted to AC, we can convert AC to DC by using a rectifier.

A rectifier is a device that permits current to flow in only one direction. A rectifier circuit can consist of one or two diodes, or a single device called a full-wave bridge rectifier consisting of four diodes. Note that this presentation is intended only to provide you with some practical information. Some basic assumptions are made to avoid a detailed discussion of unnecessary material.

I should establish here that the component we are actually discussing is called a *diode,* which acts as a one-way valve for current flow. Although the diode has other uses, we will consider its use only in a rectifier circuit. It is quite common to hear the term *rectifier* used interchangeably with the term *diode.* A *bridge rectifier* is also called a *full-wave bridge* and a *diode bridge.*

As shown in Figure 4–5, AC output would appear on an oscilloscope as a sine wave; this is shown again in Figure 4–9A. Pure DC output, as obtained from a battery, would appear as a straight line (Figure 4–9E). In DC output, there is no time or cycle, as there is in

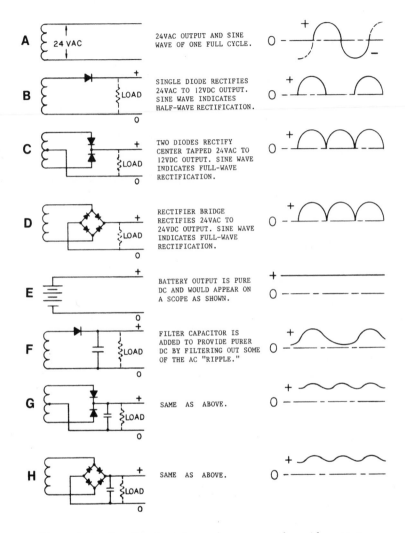

Figure 4–9. Rectification of transformer secondary side output.

AC, because DC flows in one direction continuously. By using a rectifier in the AC line, we stop the current flow in one direction. What is left is current flow in the other direction—or in one direction only. Alternating current is now changed to one-direction or direct current

(DC). Direct current maintains a constant polarity, so one side is always positive (+) and the other is zero (0) or negative (−).

Figure 4–9B shows the use of one diode in the 24VAC output side of a transformer. The resultant output is 12VDC, but as the sine wave shows, it "misses a beat" every half-cycle, or one-thirtieth of a second. This would represent a very inefficient DC power source; it is doubtful that you will ever knowingly come across or need this configuration.

Figure 4–9C shows full-wave rectification using a pair of diodes on the output of a center-tapped transformer. Assuming a 24VAC secondary output, the rectified output would be 12VDC. As shown by the sine wave, we have filled in the missing half-cycle and now have a 12VDC power source acceptable for most 12VDC electric locking devices.

Figure 4–9D shows full-wave rectification using a four-diode bridge or a rectifier bridge. Wired across a 24VAC secondary, the resultant output is 24VDC. This is acceptable for most 24VDC-operated locking devices.

When measuring the actual power, or *potential,* of the direct current, an average measurement is taken, as shown in Figure 4–10. The potential is the difference in voltage between two points. If a load of matching voltage were connected across the two points, current would flow through the load. If the two points were touched together or bridged by a conductive material (such as a screwdriver shaft), a *dead short* would occur.

The DC output is still considered "unpure" or "raw" because of the presence of AC "ripple," represented by the peaks and valleys of the sine wave. Although this raw voltage is fine for most electric locking devices, some equipment must have purer DC voltage to operate correctly.

To obtain this pureness, we have to try to straighten the sine wave so that it appears closer to pure DC, as shown by the straight line in Figure 4–9E.

A filter capacitor can be added across the output, as shown in Figures 4–9F, 4–9G, and 4–9H. A capacitor stores a small amount of voltage until it is called for. During its discharge cycle, this voltage tends to smooth out the peaks and valleys, resulting in a straighter line—or a purer DC output. There are many design considerations when using a capacitor, and errors can cause serious injury. If it is not selected or wired properly, a capacitor can explode much like a large firecracker!

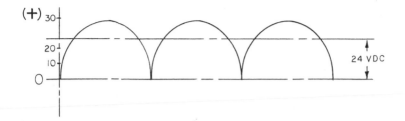

Figure 4–10.   Measurement of DC output voltage.

My recommendation for the non–electrical engineer is simply to purchase the correct DC power supply necessary for the system. All the design work will have been done by the experts, and the extra cost will be small compared to the cost of your time selecting and wiring components. Also, if you do it yourself, you might end up with a nonworking or incorrectly working power supply—and possibly a pile of roasted parts.

A typical DC power supply is shown in Figure 4–11. It is identical to an AC power supply, except for the addition of a rectifier bridge. All the same benefits apply, and it is available from the same sources.

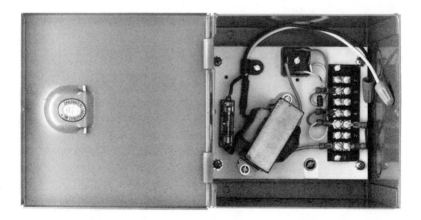

Figure 4–11.   Basic low-voltage DC power supply. This unit includes a transformer, a fuse, a rectifier bridge, a terminal block, and a grounding screw all in an electrical box. (Courtesy of Locknetics Security Products)

For low-power requirements, plug-in DC power supplies, identical to the transformer shown in Figure 4–7, are available. Once again, check local codes for restrictions on the use of any power supply.

For those of you who are knowledgeable enough about electrical hardware, using a transformer and hooking up a rectifier bridge is fine. You normally would use the hookups shown in Figures 4–9C or 4–9D. Selection of the diodes or rectifier depends on the voltage and current draw of the load to be powered. Help in this area can come from the locking device manufacturer or from a local electrical supply house. One item to remember is that there is always a voltage loss through a rectifier. Figure on a 0.7V loss when using full-wave center tap and a 1.4V loss when using the full-wave bridge.

When you are wiring in a rectifier, the simplest method is to obtain a full-wave bridge rectifier and wire it as shown in Figure 4–12A or 4–12B. Selection of the rectifier is based on the rating of the load. A big safety factor is figured in to assure reliability. It is not unusual to see a 400V, 25A rectifier in a circuit with a 24VDC, ½A load.

The rectifier is normally well marked to show where to make your connections. Notice in Figure 4–12B that only part of the full bridge is

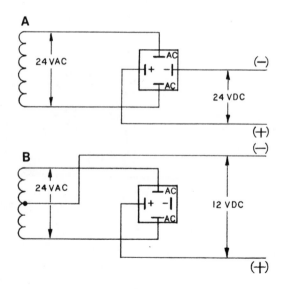

Figure 4–12. Wiring patterns for a full-wave bridge rectifier.

used. This hookup can be used only with a center-tapped transformer and results in full-wave rectified 12VDC.

REVIEW OF POWER SUPPLIES

Direct current does not reverse its polarity, as alternating current does. It always has a definite positive (+) side and negative (−) side. The simplest and purest source of DC is the battery. The most common DC voltages are 12V and 24V. Be especially careful when working with any part of the power supply that exceeds 50 volts.

Although DC can be made from AC, AC cannot be made from DC. Diodes or rectifiers are used to change AC to DC.

Power supplies should be selected to match the load requirements and to provide 25 to 50 percent more current than is necessary. Power supplies are available in many different configurations. Their main advantages are that they save time and provide a single point for wire run terminations.

POWER CONTROLLERS

The highest level of power source is designated by many different terms; throughout the text I will use the very general term *power controller*. Beyond supplying raw power, these units may provide logic to control and sequence other equipment in the system. Generally, most of these units will be providing DC power and may include standby power and regulated power. As most of these units are selected for specific applications, we will discuss their general characteristics only briefly. Your ability to select these units will increase with your experience and your recognition of the needs of the total system. Chapter 8 will give you some insight into these special needs.

We will first examine three types of output power: regulated power, special output power, and standby battery power. A power supply may be only one of these types or a combination of them. We will also discuss the power controller with logic circuitry, which also may include any or all of the three types of output power.

REGULATED POWER

As mentioned earlier, rectified DC output will be acceptable for most of the electric locking devices you will be using. These devices are tolerant of DC voltages that may run somewhat high and low, usually varying plus or minus 10 to 15 percent of rated output voltage. Occasionally, you will come across devices or equipment that require an operating voltage of closer tolerance to rating and of a "purer" DC wave form. As the security industry grows, so does the demand for more sophisticated control and monitoring equipment. Sensitive solid state alarm and access control equipment requires high-quality, stable power for proper operation.

Regulated supplies might contain filter capacitors to filter out any AC "ripple"—the remnants of AC left in the DC output after rectification. Special circuitry would be included to regulate the DC output to within a close tolerance of rating.

This regulation would also protect against any input power fluctuations. Input power is anything but stable and often will be found consistently below the 120V rating. Additional brief power disturbances can also affect the operation of sensitive equipment. The following short definitions of some of these disturbances are offered for your information, because you may hear these terms used by the electrical people:

Voltage spikes: sudden, very short duration increases in voltage. They can reach a magnitude of thousands of volts and may destroy solid state circuitry. The life of switch contacts can also be shortened by spikes.

Noise: a succession of spikes, usually of much less magnitude than a single spike. Electrical noise, though less destructive than a spike, can cause malfunctions in solid state equipment.

Voltage sags (brown-outs): drops in line voltage that can last several hours. Brown-outs can occur in a single building or an entire city. They can cause unsatisfactory operation of security devices as well as other equipment.

Voltage surges: increases in voltage above normal line power that can last fractions of a second or minutes. Although not as high in magnitude as a spike, they can still affect sensitive equipment.

Normally, any need you may have for filtered, regulated voltage will be well defined in the manufacturer's literature for the equipment for which you are providing power.

SPECIAL OUTPUT POWER

Occasionally, you may need a power supply with special output ratings. As noted in Chapter 3, some electric strikes require a high inrush current to initiate operation. With AC operation, a transformer rated high enough to handle the inrush requirements is adequate. With DC-operated strikes and electric panic devices, special power supplies can provide the inrush current by using a large capacitor in a special circuit. The inrush current is needed for a short duration only. Rather than supplying a large transformer whose full capacity would be used very little, a large capacitor supplies the short burst of energy required to start the device. A smaller transformer then supplies the holding current to the device, and the capacitor recharges for the next cycle of operation. Such power supplies are sometimes referred to as power boosters.

STANDBY BATTERY POWER

Emergency standby power is a frequently overlooked item in a security system. Power is the foundation of the security system. When power fails, security and/or life safety may be lost. For DC systems, power supplies are available that provide standby battery power when there is a line power interruption. There are several important features to watch for in a standby power supply:

1. What is the output rating in the standby mode?
2. Does the standby power supply have rechargeable batteries and a recharging circuit?
3. Is the switch-over to battery power uninterruptible?

The output of a battery is rated in amp/hours. For example, if a battery rating is 12V, 8 amp/hours, that means that a device drawing 8 amps at 12VDC would be powered for approximately one hour until battery failure. If a similar device were to draw only ½A, it would be powered for approximately sixteen hours. We always say "approximately," because several factors could affect the actual time the battery will provide full power. If the condition of the battery is not known, the time limit at full power will vary. Age, temperature, and charge status can all affect the output of the battery. Some power

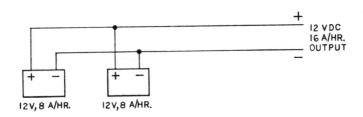

Figure 4–13. Batteries connected in parallel.

supplies are available with features that monitor the condition of the battery.

To increase the output current rating, batteries are wired together in parallel, as shown in Figure 4–13. In parallel wiring, all the positive (+) sides are wired together, and all the negative (−) sides are wired together. The output voltage is still the same as that for one battery, but the current rating is proportionately greater than that of a single battery.

Batteries of the type we ordinarily use are not available over 12VDC. To create a 24VDC output, two 12V batteries are wired in series, as shown in Figure 4–14. In series wiring, the negative electrode of one battery is connected to the positive electrode of the next battery. The output voltage is doubled, but the current rating remains the same as that of a single battery.

The chart in Figure 4–15 should give you some idea of the time limit of full power relative to the current draw of the load. The disportionate differences in time occur because battery life drops off on a curve; the higher the load, the faster the battery is drained. Always consult the manufacturer's literature for actual time/load ratings.

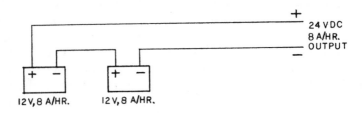

Figure 4–14. Batteries connected in series.

CURRENT DRAW (AMPS)	1/4	1/2	3/4	1	1 1/2	2
TIME AVAILABLE (HRS)	32	16	12	8	5	3

Figure 4–15. Load vs. approximate time, based on a typical 8 amp/hour gel cell battery.

Normally, these power supplies use rechargeable batteries. Look for a built-in recharging circuit, which keeps the batteries in a charged state while the unit is operating on primary power. Often, these are only "trickle" chargers. It is important to know how long it takes to fully recharge the batteries after they have been in use. It is possible that a seriously discharged battery might have to be removed and placed on a commercial battery charger.

Another important feature is the time it takes to change over from primary power to battery power. The key feature to look for is uninterruptible standby power. With this feature, when primary power fails, the standby battery power should pull in immediately. Some locking devices can withstand a very slight power interruption. The trend today, however, is toward uninterruptible service, because some high-tech equipment cannot stand even a slight interruption. A common example is the digital clock, which starts blinking if power is lost for only a second. In solid state control equipment, an entire memory could be lost in a second. Uninterruptible systems usually change over in milliseconds, allowing no loss in security or control.

Several factors must be considered in the use of standby power systems. There is some reluctance to use these systems because their cost is higher relative to standard power supplies. You may hear, "My building has emergency generators for power outages. I don't need standby power supplies." This may not always be true, however. Emergency generators in large buildings are notorious for delay time in pulling in. Some take several seconds to build up to full power before coming on line. Such a delay can cause problems in a security system.

Another common misconception is, "I have fail-secure locks. I don't need power to be locked." This is true, but they *do* need power to unlock! Such a situation may well be acceptable, but in certain cases, it could compromise life safety.

Whenever standby power is to be used, survey every aspect. The type of security situation should determine the necessary balance between security and life safety. Knowledge of the location will give you some insight into whether power outages are frequent and of long duration. Some remote locations, for example, may require enough power to last a full weekend.

POWER WITH LOGIC

A complex power controller may include some or all of the features previously covered. It also may incorporate special circuitry for specific applications within the security system. This circuitry might be solid state electronics, relay logic, or a combination of the two.

Units made up of relay circuits are still the most common. Solid state circuitry is certainly in use all over the place, but for the most part it is found in large or very sophisticated systems. Anything that can be encompassed in a relay system could certainly be done, with added features, in a solid state package. The problem with solid state, however, is its initial costs, which can be absorbed only in a mass-produced product. I will slant the discussion toward relay units because, with increased knowledge and experience, you could very well create relay logic circuits yourself. We will study the actual use of relays in more detail in Chapter 8. At this point, we will discuss why they are included in a power supply.

The relay itself is nothing more than a switch operated by electricity. It can contain multiple sets of switching contacts, and it uses very little current to operate. The contacts are used to control, coordinate, or sequence other equipment in a locking system.

Suppose we were to control a relay in a power supply with an external switch. A set of contacts belonging to that relay could, in turn, switch power on and off to a lock. A second set of contacts might switch the power source of an automatic door on or off. By using this logic circuit we could ensure that the automatic door would not work so long as the lock was "on."

Examples of the use of relays are numerous. Relays are used to control X-ray equipment, alarms, indicators, other locks in interlock systems, and on and on. Other options in relay circuitry are time delays and latching circuits with manual reset provisions. An added feature of this type of control is that the power controller can be placed near the locking device and controlled by a switch located a great distance away. The relay uses very little current and long wire runs from the control to the relay can be made on relatively small wire sizes. To be controlled directly, the lock would require much heavier wire sizes over long runs because of the higher current draw. In this manner of use, a relay can also isolate high-voltage circuits from the control switch.

Another use of the relay would be to convert different types of output signals to a signal compatible with your particular system. Depending on the type of lock you are using, you may need open or closed contacts to control it. You might be faced with contacts, or even voltage outputs, from an access control unit that are not compatible with your locking system. Instead of changing the access control system, which you probably cannot do, a relay can be controlled by these outputs. The relay contacts that match your system can then be selected to control the lock.

The prime reason for discussing these power supplies in this chapter is to inform you of their existence. Their purpose is to provide you with a ready-built system for the many different requirements you will confront in a system. When faced with complex or unusual situations, you can be sure that there is a way to provide the proper control. The best source of information would be the manufacturer of the locking device. They probably can recommend a power control unit for any situation.

TROUBLESHOOTING POWER SUPPLIES

Troubleshooting a power supply is usually quite simple. I would say that 95 percent of the problems are due to improper hookup of the system components. Normally, a hookup diagram is furnished with any power supply. If the system fails to work, or works erratically, double-check all hookup connections against the diagram. Sometimes it helps to have a second person check the hookup, as we all tend to repeat our errors when checking our own work.

Faulty external components can also cause problems. If the power supply checks out as good, the system may have to be checked to isolate a problem at some other piece of equipment. If the load is defective, it may well blow a fuse in the power supply. If you find that a fuse is blown, always try to determine the cause. It usually indicates a dead short or overload at the output terminals.

Those who have electronics backgrounds and are handy with a meter can do deeper troubleshooting. The power supply may have been supplied with a schematic or you may request one from the manufacturer. In Chapter 9, we will cover some of the basics of troubleshooting with a meter.

REVIEW OF POWER CONTROLLERS

The term *power controller* describes a power supply with a specialized feature or combination of features. Some of the available features are:

1. Regulated output power
2. Special output power
3. Emergency standby battery power
4. Logic circuitry for specific system functions

Regulated and special output power needs are defined by the specifications of the load to be powered.

Standby battery power is often overlooked in security systems. It should always be considered when designing, specifying, or installing a system. Batteries have a limited output life span, so check time and load requirements. Batteries wired in parallel increase output current, whereas batteries wired in series increase output voltage. Check to see if a standby power supply includes uninterruptibility and recharging features.

A power supply with logic circuitry for specific operations probably exists for any system requirements you will confront. Check with the lock manufacturer for availability of such units.

Selection of the power supply depends on all equipment in the system and the desired sequence of operation.

SELECTING THE POWER SOURCE

Your already increasing knowledge, and the experience you will gain, will help you decide what power supply to use. The first thing to determine is the rating of all the loads in the system. The voltages should all be the same and the current draws should be totaled. This information will tell you the power supply capacity you will need. Then you can determine whether emergency standby power is desired for DC systems.

It would be advisable, next, to list all of the devices in the system that will be controlling the lock, including key switches, card readers, fire panel, and so on. Whether you are selecting the power supply yourself or getting help, it is absolutely necessary to know the outputs of all these devices. Then list any other equipment in the system, such as monitoring devices, automatic door operators—anything that will require coordination with the locking device.

Consideration must also be given to the operation of the system, including various interlock situations, zone or individual control, fire panel tie-in, delay release and delay relocking modes, timer control, and any special requirements affecting the system.

It has always been my practice to sketch the entire system first and list the equipment required for each opening. I then write a brief description of the system operation if one has not yet been specified.

Having the system mapped out in front of you makes it easier to determine other questions that have to be asked. I always "walk" myself in and out of the doors to assure that the system operates smoothly and provides the proper security and life safety. Your sketch may also be the basis for a riser diagram. Connecting the components on the diagram and noting the number of conductors needed in each wire run will document some very valuable information.

I normally select the power supply last. A basic review of the three levels of power sources should give you an idea of the type of power supply to select:

1. *Transformers* are the simplest power supplies. They are used with simple locking systems, usually made up of an electric lock and simple dry-contact controls, such as key, pushbutton, and toggle switches. Locking devices must be rated for AC input voltage. For DC locks, a rectifier must be included within the system circuit. It is the user's responsibility to design the system hookup circuit, providing protection (fuse), tie-in points for controls and locking devices, and proper hookup information for any other components necessary to the system.

2. *Basic power supplies* are the next level up from transformers. They consist of a transformer, a fuse, a rectifier (DC units only), and a terminal block housed in a electrical box. Power supplies provide an easy method for hookup of simple locking systems, usually made up of an electric lock and simple dry-contact controls, such as key, pushbutton, and toggle switches. They are normally available in AC or DC low-voltage outputs.

3. *Power controller* is the term we use for the highest level of power supply, which is used for controlling and sequencing more complex security systems. Usually a DC unit, the power controller includes all the components of a basic power supply in addition to control relays or circuitry. It may offer a variety of options, including adjustable time delays, standby power, or special output voltages. The selection of this power supply is determined by all the other components in the system, including the release devices involved—such as a card reader, key switches, a fire panel, and so on—and any other door control equipment, such as automatic operators. Consideration must also be given to the operation of the system, including various interlock situations, central fire panel tie-in, and delayed-release systems.

5

The Control

Now that we understand the locking devices and power supplies, we must provide a means of controlling the flow of electricity between these components. A great variety of control devices are available on the market today. To avoid confusion, it is best to keep in mind that they all do the same job; that is, they all provide some sort of output that controls the locking device. The type of the control device varies only in the degree of sophistication of its operation. From a simple mechanical device such as a toggle switch to a complex electrical device such as a fingerprint reader, they all "break" or "make" an electrical path.

For the most part, we will be studying controls that provide dry-contact outputs. As we will see, these contacts simply open and close to make or break an electrical path. This type of control is by far the most common. An exception to dry contact outputs would be card, keypad, or similarly operated electronic control devices whose output is electricity. These devices are very popular with systems utilizing electric strikes. They are, in fact, the control and the power supply in one package. When selecting this type of control, consider the same factors that you use in choosing a power supply—that is, does its output provide the voltage and current needed by the locking device.

THE CONTROL MECHANISM

Controls are usually considered to be made up of two parts—the actuator and the switch or contacts. The *actuator* is the part of the control that is operated by the user to change or switch the contacts from one form or mode to another. This part may be as simple as a toggle wall switch or as complex as a mechanism operated by a card, keypad, or other means.

The *contacts* are simply metal pieces or pads made of a highly conductive material. These contacts open or close when the actuator is operated. The material used for the contacts must be highly conductive, as they are providing a path for electricity to flow, as the wire in a system does. Expensive, high-quality switches may have silver or even gold-plated contacts.

Normally, an access control device is purchased as a complete assembly. When you specify the type of operator (actuator; e.g., key switch, card reader) and the type of outputs (contact form), you have specified the entire assembly.

Table 5–1 is a fairly complete listing of all the types of control devices you may need. I have put these items into several categories in an attempt to show the level of usage of the different types. The two main categories are mechanical and electronic controls. Mechanical controls are normally the simplest; their contacts are operated by direct manual motion. In general, they are the least expensive controls, but they provide only basic, limited control over a system.

Electronic controls are more complex devices that require their own power source to remain operable. Except for preprogrammed controls, most of these devices are initially operated by some sort of manual motion, which is then converted through electronic circuitry to affect the state of the output contacts. The increasing complexity of today's security systems has created a new demand for sophisticated controls that operate and control a system in a variety of ways.

We will limit ourselves here to the basics of access controls. Covering access controls in depth would probably require an entire book. As with any of the electronic equipment we use daily, familiarity with the equipment's capabilities is all that is necessary to implement its use.

In Table 5–1, I have subdivided each of the two main types of controls into use categories. These groupings are meant to provide a general guide for selecting an appropriate device for a particular need.

Table 5–1. Mechanical and Electronic Control Devices

Type of Control	Unrestricted Use	Restricted Use	Automatic
Mechanical	Pushbutton switch Toggle switch Panic device switch Floor mat Pedal switch Break-glass station Pull station	Key switch Pushbutton-coded switch	Door status switch Equipment limit switch
Electronic	Motion detector Heat (infrared) detector Capacitance detector	Card access controls —Embossed —Hollerith —Infrared-encoded —Magnetic core (barium ferrite) —Magnetic stripe —Metallic slug (shim) —Proximity —Weigand wire Card/keypad combination Keypad control Wireless transmitter/receiver Signature reader Voice reader Fingerprint reader Hand geometry reader Retina reader Telephone dialer	Heat detector Smoke detector Gas detector Time clock

The following are brief descriptions of these subdivisions:

1. *Unrestricted use:* The use of these devices is free to all who wish to gain access through a particular opening. As is obvious with the mechanical controls, no degree of authority is necessary to operate them. Controls such as break-glass and pull stations are free to be operated by anyone but by the nature of their operation are meant to discourage their use for releasing a lock other than during an emergency. Unrestricted electronic controls would be programmed to release a lock whenever a person entered an area in close proximity to the opening. An example of this type of device is a detector that reacts to movement or heat within its range to operate an automatic door.

2. *Restricted use:* The use of these devices would require that a person be authorized to do so. Special knowledge of a code or possession of a card or key would be necessary to gain access to an opening. Some of today's high-security devices even require verification of the user through such personal identification as fingerprint, voice, or retina recognition.

3. *Automatic control:* Any device that releases a lock according to some preprogrammed condition would be considered an automatic control. In mechanical controls, some sort of switch might be wired in such a manner as to lock or unlock a door whenever another door or piece of equipment was used. This type of operation is popular in systems such as door interlocks, X-ray machine interlocks, and elevator door control. Automatic electronic controls are programmed to react to conditions such as fire and smoke to control a lock or group of locks. Automatic time switches are programmed for automatic lock–unlock cycles during certain hours of the day. They may also include provisions that skip entire unlocking cycles during long time periods such as weekends.

Note that I have listed eight types of card access controls in Table 5–1. As noted earlier, detailing every access control device would require another book. It would be best for you to rely on manufacturers' literature for further information on this subject.

Figures 5–1 through 5–6 show some of the control devices listed in Table 5–1. A great variety of control devices are available; consult manufacturers' literature for available features.

Figure 5–1. Key switch: mechanical control, restricted use. (Courtesy of Security Engineering, Inc.)

CONTACT FORMS

It is the contacts within the switch or device that do the work of controlling the electrical energy. Because of this, contacts are rated according to the amount of current they can switch. Most of the controls you will be using will be rated high enough to handle low-voltage electric locking equipment.

A typical contact rating might be 6A at 120VAC. This indicates that the contact can carry 6 amps of AC current at 120 volts. A

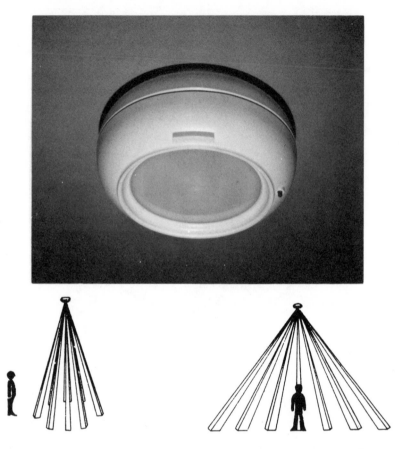

Figure 5–2. Passive infrared sensor: electronic control, unrestricted use. (Courtesy of Pulnix America, Inc.)

question arises regarding how much current this contact will carry at, say, 24VDC. To calculate this, you would have to be well versed in electrical engineering. If a contact is rated at a specific voltage, that does not mean it will carry the rated amperage at a different voltage, especially crossing from AC to DC. If the switch is not marked with a voltage rating close to the voltage of the load you are controlling, consult the manufacturer's data sheet for additional rating information.

Figure 5–3. Card readers and associated equipment: electronic control, restricted use. (Courtesy of Synergistics, Inc.)

The *contact form* is the configuration of the contacts within the device. Figure 5–7 shows many of the available contact forms. The word *form* and the single-letter or double-letter designation are electrical terms. You will most often find contact configurations identified by the more descriptive multiple-letter designations.

Before defining designations, I should clarify several of the terms used in the definitions. *Pole* refers to the moving portion of the contact; it is also sometimes referred to as the *swinger* or *common* of the switch. *Single pole* and *double pole* are the most common, but it is possible to have additional poles on switches. The terms *normally open* and *normally closed* usually cause the most confusion. *Normal* refers to the natural state of the contacts, with no external force influencing them. Suppose that you purchase a normally open plunger-type door status switch. When this switch is mounted in a door jamb and the door is closed, the depressed plunger causes the switch to close. The influence of the door causes the contacts to become closed. Although this may be the normal condition of the system, it is *not* the normal condition of the contacts. The contacts would

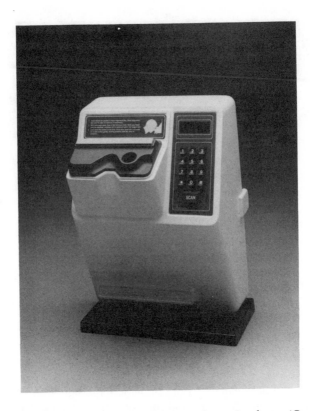

Figure 5–4.   Retina reader: electronic control, restricted use. (Courtesy of Eyedentify, Inc.)

be described as "normally open–held closed." A common practice, in lieu of using this term, is to show the contacts with the swinger in its opposite from "normal" position (see Figure 5–8).

Notice that in Figure 5–8 the switch is shown closed but is labeled NO, or normally open. This is where most of the confusion lies, as people would tend to label it normally closed (NC). This is wrong because if you were to use a switch marked with both NO and NC contacts, you would surely wire the wrong contact.

It is wise to study the system hookup drawings carefully to determine how the switch is actually wired. Most drawings do not label the contacts with such designations as SPNO or SPDT. Contact sets are

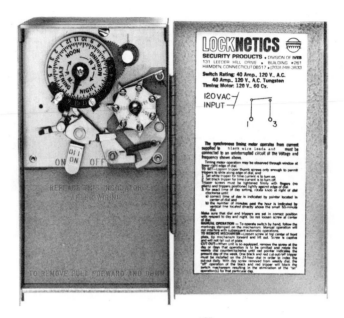

Figure 5–5. Time clock switch: electronic control, automatic. (Courtesy of Locknetics Security Products)

usually labeled as shown in Figure 5–9 (where C means common). The switch itself should be marked in the same manner.

The following are definitions of the terms for the contact forms shown in Figure 5–7.

> **SPST:** single pole, single throw. The switch has only one moving contact and one stationary contact; it is available either normally open or normally closed.
> **NO:** normally open. The circuit will be open until the switch actuator is operated.
> **NC:** normally closed. The circuit will be closed until the switch actuator is operated.
> **SPDT:** single pole, double throw. The switch has one moving contact and two stationary contacts (NO and NC); when operated, the contacts reverse states.
> **DP:** double pole. It is available in single throw and double throw

Figure 5–6. Smoke and flame detectors: electronic control, automatic. (Courtesy of Gamewell Corp.)

configurations; it allows for two separate circuits to be operated simultaneously from one switch.

DB: double breaking. This type of configuration (forms X, Y, Z) provides the same circuits as forms A, B, and C except that when activated, the pole makes or breaks a circuit from two contact points. Form Z can be converted to form C by adding a jumper to one side, as shown in Figure 5–10.

The five contact forms shown in Figure 5–11 are the most commonly used. It would be wise to study these configurations carefully, as they are apt to show up in systems you will work with.

When only an NO or NC contact is needed, it is common practice to use an SPDT switch. This switch is often more readily obtainable, and the side of the contact set that is not being used is always there if needed later.

OPERATING MODES

Two operating modes are available for switching actions: *maintained action* (also called alternate action), and *momentary action*. Momen-

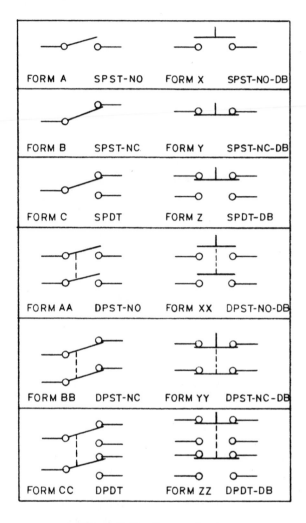

Figure 5–7.   Contact forms.

tary action can also include a third or optional mode called *time-delayed action.*

On mechanical switches, the actuator or operator is selected to provide the mode that will affect the opening and closing of the

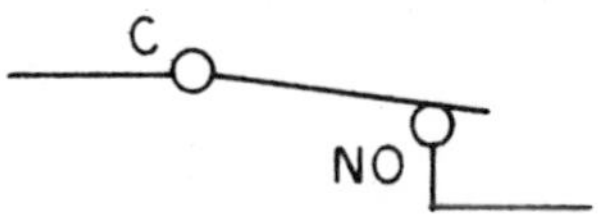

Figure 5–8. Normally open contacts shown in a "held-closed" state.

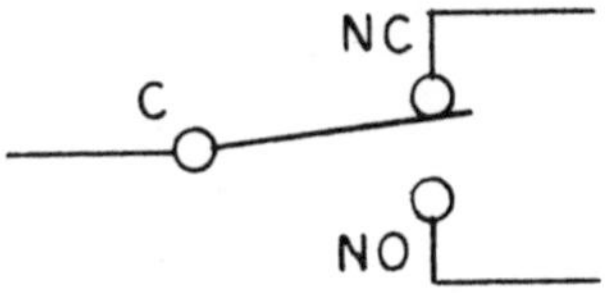

Figure 5–9. Contact labeling.

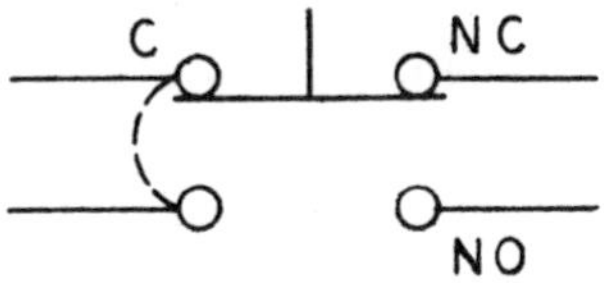

Figure 5–10. Converting form Z contacts to form C contacts.

contacts. Maintained switching is most commonly associated with pushbutton, toggle, and key switches. The term *maintained* indicates that whenever a switch is operated and the contacts change state, that change remains in effect until the switch is operated again. A common light switch is a good example of maintained switching. When the toggle of the switch is flipped from the off position to the on position, a normally open contact closes and remains closed. This completes a circuit, sending electricity through the contacts to a light bulb. You must operate that toggle again to return those contacts to the open position, thus opening the path of the circuit and turning off the light.

All mechanical switches are available with momentary action; some, such as floor mat switches, are available *only* with momentary action. The term *momentary* indicates that whenever a switch is operated and the contacts change state, that change remains in effect only while the operator of the switch is held in the position to which it was moved. A good example of momentary switching is the door bell switch to a house or apartment. This type of switch would have normally open contacts wired in the circuit with the bell and transformer. When the button of the switch is depressed, the contacts close, and the completed circuit allows the electricity to flow to the bell. The bell will continue to ring so long as the button is depressed. Once you have taken your finger off the button, the contacts return to open and the bell ceases to ring.

Some momentary switches may offer an option called delayed action or time delay. This feature may utilize a mechanical, pneumatic, or electronic device to delay the return of the contacts to their normal condition. Time-delay devices are usually adjustable, with a typical range of 0 to 60 seconds. Long delay times are normally accomplished by using clock-type timers.

Electronic controls with output contacts are most likely to have momentary action switches, with or without time delay. As noted in the list of electronic controls in Table 5–1, these devices can be operated by several different methods. The internal electronics decipher whether a card or code is valid and cause the output contacts to change state. The momentary action is necessary so that the device will return to normal, allowing its use by the next person desiring access through the door. Time-delay action is a commonly available option on these access control devices. If the device is not located immediately next to the opening, so that a person could push open the door before removing the card, the delay holds the output contacts in their changed state for several seconds. This allows the user to get to the door before it relocks.

CONTROL SELECTION

When selecting the proper controls for entering and exiting an opening, you must consider many things. Poorly designed systems may cause otherwise honest people to attempt to circumvent or damage the control device. You must determine what will provide adequate security and life safety for each opening. You must also resolve what codes will allow on certain openings.

The access side and the egress side of the opening should be treated separately. The more controlled the access or egress is at an opening,

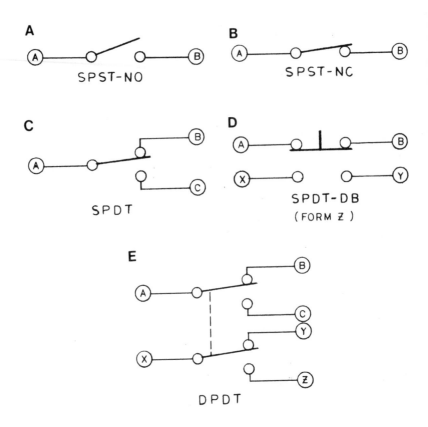

Figure 5–11. Common contact forms. (A) Single pole, single throw, normally open switch keeps circuit A-B open. This could be used in a system with a fail-secure lock. When the switch is operated, contact closes, completing circuit A-B. Electricity would flow to lock, causing it to release. (B) Single pole, single throw, normally closed switch keeps circuit A-B closed. This could be used in a system with a fail-safe lock. When the switch is operated, contact opens, breaking circuit A-B. Electricity would cease to flow to lock, causing it to release. (C) Single pole, double throw switch provides a closed circuit, A-B, and an open circuit, A-C. This could be used in a system with a fail-safe lock in circuit A-B and a light in circuit A-C. When the switch is operated, circuit A-B opens, releasing the lock, and circuit A-C closes, turning the light on. The lock and light would have to be rated for the same voltage. (D) Single pole, double throw, form Z switch provides two separated circuits—one closed (A-(B) and one open (X-Y). This switch could operate the same as the system in

the more inconvenient it will be for people to use that opening. This may be a desirable feature. Keep in mind that you cannot provide both controlled and unrestricted controls for *simultaneous* use at an opening. Although both types of controls may be present, one will have to be disabled or shunted out of the system when the other is in use.

Passage may be restricted on one side but not the other. It may be necessary to use a restricted control on the access side and an unrestricted device for free egress from the exit side. On certain designated egress doors or fire exit doors, codes will dictate the types of controls that may be used. When using restricted controls, it is also necessary to determine the level of control desired.

Traffic patterns, accessibility for the handicapped, and varying levels of authorized use will influence the type and sophistication of the control device. The quality of the device may also vary by the type of facility involved. Frequency of use, vulnerability to vandalism, and weather all play a part in the selection process.

Additional equipment may be added to a system if visual and/or audible contact is necessary at the opening. Examples of such equipment include closed-circuit television (CCTV), intercoms, and telephones.

Because of the rapid development of the electronic access control market, there is some confusion regarding the purpose and use of much of the equipment available today. The tendency is to provide either too much or too little security for the system requirements.

The following are some of the questions that should be resolved when you are selecting control devices:

---

part C (SPDT) except that the lock and light could be of different voltages. Each circuit is totally separated and could be wired to two different low-voltage power supplies. As shown in Figure 5–10, tying line *A* to line *X* will give you an SPDT switch that provides an NO and NC switch controlling one single circuit. (E) Double pole, double throw switch provides a set of NO and NC contacts for controlling two separate circuits. The swingers of each contact set are mechanically attached together, as indicated by the dotted line. Whenever the switch is operated, both contact sets change position simultaneously. When shown on a drawing, the contact sets may be drawn in separate locations for convenience. They will be identified as belonging to one switch; that is, the switch may be labeled S1 and the contact sets labeled S1-A and S1-B.

1. *What service does the opening provide? Public access* may require a day/night mode control switch to facilitate free access during certain hours. *Traffic control* may require free access from one side but not the other. You might use a double-egress interior opening, with each side of each door treated differently; each leaf may be controlled individually or they may be controlled as a pair. For a *private entrance*, the sophistication of the control device can vary greatly. Such an entrance might require a printed record of usage. With *automatic operators*, control of the lock must be coordinated with the automatic operator to ensure smooth operation of the door. In a typical situation, there might be a restricted device (card reader, coded keypad, etc.) on the outside and a motion detector or floor mat to provide uninhibited egress from the other side. In a *stair tower*, controls will be affected by local codes governing specific situations. Mantrap or sallyport *interlocks* can cover a variety of situations. Controls have to be coordinated with power supply logic and door status monitoring.

2. *Should access be restricted?* As indicated in the preceding paragraph, controls can vary greatly, from a simple key switch to some type of reader with a printout option. Added sophistication may include such options as an "anti-passback" feature, which requires that a card be reused to exit the door before it can again be used to reenter. This control ensures that the card cannot be "passed back" to other persons to gain unauthorized entrance. Day/night selection of the control devices may also be desired. By shunting out the restricted control device during the day, a simpler unrestricted device may be included in the system.

3. *Should egress be restricted?* In interlock situations, some predetermined condition may have to exist before egress is allowed. This condition may be determined by the status of other doors in the system or equipment such as X-ray machines. Perimeter exit doors may also be allowed some degree of restriction. Chapter 5 of National Fire Protection Association (NFPA) 101—Life Safety Code details a delayed unlocking sequence that allows some degree of security without seriously compromising life safety. You would have to check with the authority having jurisdiction to see whether such an arrangement is allowable.

4. *What is the frequency of use of the opening?* When specifying the controls for a system, it is important to know the anticipated traffic flow in the area. When actual figures are not available, a rough

estimate may be used. Internal doors may average four to ten openings a day by each employee or tenant in the building. Naturally, main entrances will be used much more frequently. Appendix B provides a chart for frequency of operation for several types of openings. An estimate of a hundred or more operations a day would indicate the need for a high-quality, heavy-duty control. Once again, it may be desirable to use a maintained unlocking cycle during heavy traffic hours. This can be accomplished by a simple on/off switch or, automatically, by a timer control.

5. *Is the opening a designated egress or fire exit door?* For such openings, it is again necessary to refer to local codes for guidance. Chapter 5 of NFPA 101—Life Safety Code provides excellent information on the allowable operation of certain controls. In several instances, the code states that, on the egress side of certain openings, under certain conditions, the release of the lock shall not require special knowledge or effort and the method of operation must be obvious, even in darkness. These statements can lead to some very heated debates regarding which devices are allowable and which are not. Many people find it difficult to read the code book, but when it is treated as another source of information, it can produce a wealth of knowledge pertaining to methods and reasons for egress control. When specifying hardware for designated egress or fire exit doors, a knowledge of the codes is mandatory.

6. *Is handicapped accessibility a requirement?* Most of the time, handicapped accessibility will be determined during the architect's planning stages. Accessibility is associated with automatic doors in the majority of cases. Your concern might only be with the size, style, and location of the control devices. Buttons and push plates may be larger than normal and located lower than usual. The American National Standards Institute (ANSI) publication A117.1 can provide more insight into handicapped accessibility requirements.

7. *Does the type of traffic dictate special consideration?* Control devices may be selected to service openings frequented by a specific category of people. For example, in areas or buildings used primarily by the elderly or disabled, controls may be similar to those covered by handicapped accessibility requirements, and detention and juvenile facilities may require heavy-duty, tamper-resistant controls.

8. *Is delayed relocking desirable?* This is a frequently overlooked question during selection of the control device. For practical purposes,

we will assume that the controls are to be in momentary action mode; that is, the contacts return to normal after the device has been activated. This type of control eliminates the problem of the control being left in the unlocked position inadvertently. If the control is located directly adjacent to or on the strike jamb face of the frame, a delay may not be necessary. When the user operates the control with one hand, the door may be opened with the other hand. This mode of egress may be desirable to reduce the chance of someone following an authorized person through the opening. If unrestricted controls are used, a delay may be warranted, especially at openings where the users are apt to be carrying items through on a regular basis and may not have two free hands. If any control is located away from the immediate door area, a time delay should be specified. Time delays are available on many control devices, including pushbuttons, key switches, and card readers. The delay is usually adjustable, commonly from 0 to 60 seconds. If a specific control is not available with a time-delay feature, the locking device or power supply may be available with this option.

9.   *Is there a budget?* As with anything else, economics will play a role in the selection process. The amount that can be spent on the system must be considered, as well as what is really needed for a specific application. Good practice would not justify treating a remote warehouse door like a computer room entrance. The expense of sophisticated access control equipment should be sufficient motivation to determine the real requirements of an opening.

10.   *What else must be considered in the selection process?* Adding options and including mounting hardware can enhance the control system. Some controls are available with optional indicator lights to monitor the status of the lock. Without monitoring indicators at the door, there is no way to tell whether or not the lock is in a secure state. Pushbutton controls may also offer a variety of actuator colors and sizes. Engraved or silkscreened legends—such as "Push to Release," "Push to Exit"—can also add to the system. To facilitate installation, mounting hardware should be specified or supplied. These items may include weather-resistant covers or enclosures, mortised or surface electrical boxes, and desktop housings. Tamper-resistant attaching hardware may also be included if it is not supplied as standard.

Once all these elements are considered, equipment may be selected to provide the desired results. Because of the great variety of control devices on the market today, it would be wise to create a small library or file of the various types of equipment.

TROUBLESHOOTING

It will usually be fairly obvious if a control device is defective or has failed. Controls that have open or closed dry contacts can be disconnected from the system and easily checked with a meter. If a meter is not available, replacing the control with a jumper wire can isolate the problem. If a locking device fails to operate when the control is used but responds when operated manually by a jumper, chances are that the switch is defective. Controls with voltage outputs can also be checked with the meter.

Other items that can affect the control system are the door and the door hardware. The door should be equipped with an operating closer to ensure that it closes fully after being used. A door that is hinge-bound, sagging, or warped will also hinder correct operation.

REVIEW

The control device provides a means of controlling the flow of electricity through a locking device. Basic controls generally provide an open and/or closed dry contact as an output to make or break a circuit. In some instances, the control device can provide a voltage output to operate an electric lock directly.

Controls are generally made up of two components: the actuator and the switch or contacts. The contacts are made of a highly conductive material. Controls can be either mechanical or electrical. Electrical controls require their own power source. Control devices can provide unrestricted use, restricted use, or automatic control.

Switch contacts are rated for the maximum voltage and current they can carry. Contacts are available in many forms or configurations. *Normally open* and *normally closed* refer to the natural state of the contacts when they are under no external influence.

Switch actuators are available in two actions or modes: momentary and maintained. Momentary switching can include a time-delay option, delaying the return of the contacts to "normal."

Before selecting the control for a specific system, you should survey the system conditions and requirements. Troubleshooting of control devices can usually be done with a meter.

6

The Conductor

The conductor is the electrical wire or cable that provides a complete path for electric current to flow in a system. The use of wire in a security system is so commonplace that it is often taken for granted. Because it is not a highly visible item, it is not given the same attention as the other system components. However, you should spend as much time selecting and planning the wire for a system as you spend on any other component.

Most wiring work is done by the electrical contractor or electrical project engineer. I am including a discussion of the conductor here because it is important that everyone involved with the system be aware of the wiring requirements.

TYPES OF WIRE

The type of wire in which we are most interested is stranded copper hookup wire, usually in sizes between 10 and 26 gauge. I will mention other types of wire briefly for reference only.

Although hookup wire is available as either solid or stranded conductor, stranded wire is the accepted standard for system hookup

Table 6–1. Wire and Cable Types

Type	Description	Use
Single conductor solid (bell wire)	Solid core, insulated	House wiring (low-voltage bell circuits), internal construction of electrical equipment
Single conductor stranded (hookup)	Stranded core, insulated	Hookup of electrical system components, internal wiring of electronic equipment
Twisted pair	Two conductors, insulated and intertwined around each other	Sometimes used for systems hookup; provides some shielding from outside "noise" interference
Parallel (zip cord)	Two parallel conductors, insulated	Short AC power runs (lamp, radio, etc.); one side of insulation may be ribbed to identify polarity
Telephone wire	Four conductors, solid, insulated	Small-gauge wire used for telephone systems
Coaxial cable	Inner conductor, solid or stranded, insulated; outer braided shield acts as second conductor, with or without insulation	Audio equipment
Nonmetallic, sheathed (Romex)	Two or three conductors bundled together, solid, insulated	Building wiring
Armored (BX)	Two or more conductors in flexible steel conduit, solid, insulated	Building wiring

wire. Solid wire is most often used in circuits that are not subject to movement, such as house wiring, bell wiring, transformer winding, and the like. Table 6–1 is a description and use chart for wire and cable types.

Stranded wire is made up of several small-diameter wires twisted together to form one larger-diameter conductor. This type of construction allows more flexibility without breaking than solid wire.

Wire is given a gauge number to classify it by its size or thickness. American wire gauge (AWG) is the most common measurement for electrical wire size. Figure 6–1 shows a comparison of wire sizes.

It should be noticed that the lower the wire gauge number, the larger the wire diameter. Stranded wire of a specific gauge is slightly larger in diameter than solid wire of the same gauge, but they both have the same current carrying capability because they both have the same number of circular mils. A circular mil is the cross-sectional area of a circle that is 0.001 inch, or 1 mil, in diameter. The cross-sectional area of any round wire (metal area only) is found by squaring the diameter in mils, or thousandths of an inch (multiply the diameter by itself).

The wire sizes you will come across most often in low-voltage wiring will be 18 and 16 gauge. Smaller sizes are used mostly for manufacturing of electrical equipment; larger sizes are used for high-voltage building wiring.

Most of the wire you will be using will be made of copper. Some manufacturers offer copper-coated aluminum wire as a way to save money on wiring. It is best to avoid using this type of wire as it requires a heavier gauge to achieve the same conductivity as copper wire. The level of conductivity of some metals is shown in Table 6–2. The high expense of silver and gold limit their use to military and computer applications.

Figure 6–1. Diameters of electrical wire without insulation.

Table 6–2. Relative Conductivity of Some Metals

Metal	Electric Conductivity
Silver	100.0
Copper	97.6
Gold	76.6
Aluminum	63.0
Platinum	14.4
Tungsten	14.0

All hookup wire is covered by some type of insulated coating to prevent it from touching other conductive materials and causing short circuits.

SELECTION OF WIRE

The most important concern in selecting wire is ensuring that the thickness or gauge of the wire is of sufficient size to carry the amount of current that must pass through it. All wire offers some resistance to current flow. The larger the wire diameter, the less resistance it offers and the more easily it passes current. Table 6–3 shows resistance values for copper wire.

Table 6–3. Resistance of Copper Wire at 68°F

Size (AWG)	Diameter (in.)	Area (cir. mils)	Weight (lb. per 1,000 ft.)	Resistance (ohms per 1,000 ft.)
10	0.102	10,380.0	31.43	1.00
12	0.081	6,530.0	19.77	1.59
14	0.064	4,107.0	12.43	2.53
16	0.051	2,583.0	7.82	4.02
18	0.040	1,624.0	4.92	6.39
20	0.032	1,022.0	3.09	10.15
22	0.025	642.4	1.95	16.14
24	0.020	404.0	1.22	25.67
26	0.016	254.1	0.77	40.81

If the wire is too small for a particular application, high resistance will result in heating of the wire and a loss of power (voltage drop). Voltage drop must be held to a minimum for efficient operation of the load. For example, power loss in an indicator light will cause the light's glow to dim. Voltage drop in an electromagnet or solenoid may cause it to function poorly or not at all. Resistance increases as the wire gets longer or smaller. Generally, as wire runs get longer, the wire size must be increased to prevent excessive voltage drops.

There are several methods of calculating voltage drop. One basic formula is as follows:

$$VD = \frac{2LRI}{1,000}$$

where VD = voltage drop

L = one-way length of wire, in feet

R = conductor resistance, in ohms per 1,000 feet

I = current draw of load, in amps

Calculating the correct wire size can be time-consuming. Wire length and current draw would be known values, and resistance can be found in a table such as Table 6–3, using an estimated wire size. After the calculation, the answer (VD) should not be more than 5 percent of the voltage rating of the load. Generally, a voltage drop of 10 percent could be tolerated, but 5 percent leaves a good safety factor and is the figure used in National Electrical Code (NEC) calculations.

Another method would be to plug in a specific percentage of voltage drop, calculate resistance, and select the wire size using a table similar to Table 6–3. Let us assume that a 5 percent voltage drop is acceptable, L = 250 feet, and I = .25A at 24V. First, reduce the formula as follows:

$$1.2 \ (5\% \ of \ 24V) = \frac{2LRI}{1,000}$$

$$1,200 = 2LRI$$

$$600 = LRI$$

$$R = \frac{600}{LI}$$

$$R = \frac{600}{250 \times .25}$$

$R = 9.6$ (conductor resistance in ohms)

Looking at Table 6–3, we find that the closest resistance under 9.6 is 6.39, indicating that 18 gauge wire could be used.

As I have indicated, these calculations are normally done by the electrical contractor or engineer. When you must select wire, you can usually find helpful tables for wire selection in manufacturers' literature. I have provided Table 6–4 for this purpose. The recommended wire sizes in the table are based on an allowable voltage drop of no more than 5 percent. Using one wire size higher than that indicated in the table would give you even less of a voltage drop. This would be ideal, as the less drop there is, the more efficiently the system will operate. On the other hand, too large a wire size can add unnecessary expense to the job. Although I have indicated the use of wire sizes less than 18 AWG in some instances, it is good practice to consider 18 AWG a minimum size.

All the wire you will use will have some sort of thermoplastic insulation. Using "approved" wire (UL, CSA, etc.) will ensure proper insulation for the type of wire selected. Once again, local codes may specify allowable types and ratings of wire. Articles 720 and 725 of the National Electrical Code cover wiring for low-voltage circuits.

In many cases, it will be advantageous to use two or more conductors grouped together in a single cable. Always select cable with color-coded conductors. When hooking up components, always mark the color of each conductor on the hookup drawing. This will provide a record of where each wire goes if troubleshooting becomes necessary. I have seen jobs where only one color of wire was used for hookup, making troubleshooting impossible!

As noted earlier, stranded copper wire, 18 AWG minimum, is an acceptable norm for system wiring. Selection of other types of wire depends on the application and the user's preference, so long as applicable codes are not violated.

Table 6–4.   Wire Size Selection

Total One-Way Length of Wire Run (ft.)	Load Current @ 24V							
	1/4A	1/2A	3/4A	1A	1 1/4A	1 1/2A	2A	3A
100	24	20	18	18	16	16	14	12
150	22	18	16	16	14	14	12	10
200	20	18	16	14	14	12	12	10
250	18	16	14	14	12	12	12	10
300	18	16	14	12	12	12	10	—
400	18	14	12	12	10	10	—	—
500	16	14	12	10	10	—	—	—
750	14	12	10	10	—	—	—	—
1,000	14	10	10	—	—	—	—	—
1,500	12	10	—	—	—	—	—	—

Total One-Way Length of Wire Run (ft.)	Load Current @ 12V							
	1/4A	1/2A	3/4A	1A	1 1/4A	1 1/2A	2A	3A
100	20	18	16	14	14	12	12	10
150	18	16	14	12	12	12	10	—
200	16	14	12	12	10	10	—	—
250	16	14	12	10	10	10	—	—
300	16	12	12	10	10	—	—	—
400	14	12	10	—	—	—	—	—
500	14	10	10	—	—	—	—	—
750	12	10	—	—	—	—	—	—
1,000	10	—	—	—	—	—	—	—
1,500	10	—	—	—	—	—	—	—

Some users prefer solid wire because it doesn't fray and is easily terminated. Conversely, stranded wire is more flexible, does not break as easily, and crimps better than solid wire.

I have referred to the National Electrical Code several times regarding wiring. The NEC is an accepted guide for safe wiring practices, but it does not become law until it is legally adopted as a local code. "Local" code may be state, town, or county code. Local authorities may adopt the NEC in whole or in part or may even write their own code. Prominent examples of local codes that vary from the NEC are those in Chicago and Pittsburgh.

When doing any electrical work or selecting wire for a job, be sure to check with local authorities for the code requirements regarding wire in that jurisdiction.

WIRE CONNECTIONS

Wires must be properly connected to each other, to switches, to terminal boards, and to other devices. Although this is easy to do, it is often done incorrectly. Anyone who works with wiring should be thoroughly familiar with connectors, splicing, and soldering. A poorly made connection can cause all sorts of problems in a system that are often difficult to locate.

The first step in making any connection is to remove some of the insulation from the end of the wire. The stripped end of the wire should also be checked for cleanliness. When using a knife, never cut straight through the insulation. The knife blade should be held almost flat against the wire to avoid cutting into the metal. Slide the blade along the wire, removing insulation to the end. The length of insulation removed will depend on the type of termination to be made. Clean the exposed wire by scraping or brushing with emery cloth.

An easier way to strip wires is to use a wire stripper, as shown in Figure 6–2A. Investing in a good wire stripper can save you a lot of time and ensure that a proper strip has been made.

Three methods of terminating wires are splicing, connectors, and soldering. Splicing will be mentioned only briefly, as you should not need to use this method. In many cases, the NEC does not allow spliced wires, and it is good practice to avoid them. When splicing is necessary, the splice must be as strong and as good a conductor as the original wire. The splice must also be properly insulated when finished.

Solderless connectors are the most often used electrical hardware for terminating wires. The most common types used in low-voltage wiring are screw terminals, crimp terminals, and wire nuts. Most of these connectors are designed to take wires stripped to the proper length, with no additional insulation required.

Screw terminals are provided on many electrical devices, especially power supplies. The end of the wire need only be stripped and bent to

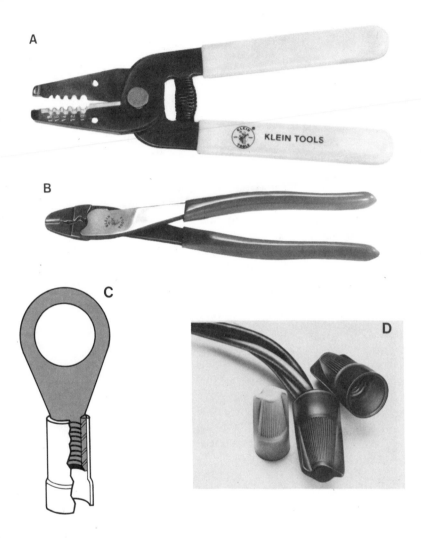

Figure 6–2. Tools and connectors. (A) Wire-stripping tool. (Courtesy of Klein Tools, Inc.) (B) Crimping tool. (Courtesy of Klein Tools, Inc.) (C) Typical solderless (crimped) connector. (Courtesy of Klein Tools, Inc.) (D) Solderless wire connectors (wire nuts). (Courtesy of Heyco Molded Products, Inc.)

form a hook, which is placed under the screw head, with the open side facing in the same direction that the screw tightens. When using stranded wire, the ends should be twisted tightly together before being placed under the screw head. It should also be noted that the NEC prohibits more than one wire under a screw terminal. Multiple wires can be connected by a wire nut. A single wire leaving the wire nut can then be connected to the screw terminal.

Crimp terminals are another popular wire termination. These connectors are generally found in factory-wired electrical equipment, but they can be used in the field with a proper crimping tool. Figures 6–2B and 6–2C show a basic crimping tool and a typical crimp terminal. Crimp terminals are available to take different wire sizes, and some will handle more than one conductor. Types include ring tongue, spade, flag, hook, blade, quick-connect, and offset; all are available insulated and noninsulated. Crimp connectors work best with stranded wire, as it crushes down better than solid wire. Properly sized and crimped, the connection will be as electrically and mechanically sound as a solder connection.

Wire nuts (Figure 6–2D) are one of the most popular connecting devices. One type has a metal insert with a set screw that is tightened against the wires; a plastic cover is screwed over the insert to provide insulation. The other, more common type is one piece with an internal tapered thread. The wires to be connected are simply laid parallel to each other. The wire nut is screwed on over the wires, twisting them together. If the ends of the wires have been properly stripped, no bare wire will be visible. Always use the right size connector for the number and size of the wires you are connecting. Make sure it is UL-listed for your intended purpose.

Soldering is rarely, if ever, used to make field connections. The odds of making a bad solder connection are very high, and it is often difficult to detect a bad solder joint. In most cases, the NEC prohibits soldered connections.

In some situations, you may have to make solder connections inside electronic equipment or, occasionally, to attach hookup wire to solder terminals on electronic devices. If the need should arise, a dependable solder connection requires the following:

1. Mechanical soundness of the parts to be joined
2. Clean joining surfaces

3. Application of an oxide-removing flux
4. Application of heat and solder (heat the joint, not the solder; use a heat sink on electronic parts)

After soldering, a good joint will have a shiny appearance. A "cold" solder joint will have a dull appearance, which indicates that not enough heat was applied to make the solder bond properly. A cold solder joint doesn't provide a good mechanical or electrical connection. The cold joint must be cut out and the wire restripped and resoldered.

Selecting the proper solder is also an important factor. Three grades of soft solder (an alloy of tin and lead) are generally used for electrical/electronic work: 40-60, 50-50, and 60-40 solder. (The first figure is the percentage of tin; the second is the percentage of lead.) Although 60-40 solder is more expensive, it flows more easily (melting at 361°F), takes less time to harden, and generally makes it easier to do a good soldering job.

In addition to the solder, there must be a flux to remove any oxide film on the metals being joined. A noncorrosive rosin flux may be included in the hollow core of the solder.

CONDUCTING DEVICES

Although we have discussed wires that provide a continuous path for electrical power and devices for connecting wires to each other to continue the path, there will be places that present barriers or gaps that wires cannot pass through or over. These situations require additional devices to bridge these obstacles, allowing a continuous electrical path. Several different products are available for this purpose, including contact sets, door cords, electric hinges and pivots, and power transfers.

Most of these devices contain wires that are rated to carry a specific voltage and current. The same principles covered in the discussion of wire selection apply, except that there is usually a very limited selection of available wire sizes. The size of wire used in these devices is restricted by the construction of the device.

Normally, only two conditions will require the use of these devices. One condition would be an electric locking device mounted in or on a door, requiring that power be brought from the frame to the door.

This situation would require the transfer of whatever current the lock requires and would need a power transfer device with large enough wire to do so. Usually, a transfer device with large enough conductors is available for the normally low lock current. In some cases, the transfer device may have up to eight small conductors, which individually can handle only low current draws. It is acceptable in a pinch to gang the conductors into two "cables," providing two single conductors that can handle heavier currents. This practice should not be done by conjecture, however, as the gauge of the "new" wire you have created is based on the total area (circular mils) of the smaller wires used to form it.

For example, as shown in Table 6–3, 24 AWG wire has an area of 404 circular mils. If we were to twist four 24 gauge wires together, the total area would be 1,616 circular mils. Checking the area column in Table 6–3, we would find that we have created a single wire equivalent to an 18 gauge conductor.

The other condition requiring an additional conducting device would be the transfer of a signal from a switch mounted on a door, such as a monitor switch in a lock or exit device. The switch is usually carrying only the load of a light or relay and normally can be serviced by small-diameter conductors.

Of all the conducting devices, contact sets are the least used today. It is doubtful that you could find a manufacturer still offering this product. The contact set consisted of a metal plate with two spring-loaded conductive pins protruding from it. Two wires from the hinge side of the frame would be attached to the back of each pin bushing and the plate would be mortised into the frame. Two wires from the door would be attached to two conductive pads on a matching plate. This plate would be mortised into the hinge edge of the door. When the door closed, the two spring pins would come in contact with the conductive pads. This provided two paths for the power to flow through. The ease with which these devices could be tampered with, and unreliable continuity due to dirt and oxidation, caused them to fall out of favor in recent years.

Door cords are a popular product for transferring power from the frame to the door. The type shown in Figure 6–3 is used to provide a little more resistance to vandalism. Door cords are usually available with two or four conductors and with a choice of cord lengths. The greatest drawback to their use is vulnerability to tampering because of

Figure 6–3. Concealed door cord, available with four conductors and optional built-in door status switch. (Courtesy of Sentrol, Inc.)

their high exposure, but their relatively low cost makes them popular for low-security applications.

Electric hinges and pivots are the most practical and reliable means of transferring power while maintaining security. Figures 6–4 and 6–5 illustrate several of these devices. Although higher in cost than other devices, they offer excellent tamper-resistance. Some of the available devices are designed to carry the weight of the door. Others are not load-bearing hardware and are used as power transfers only. Electric hinges are normally mounted in the center position of the door and frame. The wires are continuous conductors, running through one leaf, around the barrel, and through the other leaf. The number of conductors varies from two to eight, and the wires are usually available in sizes from 26 to 22 gauge. The current-carrying capacity ranges from ½ to 3 amps, and there is generally no need to be concerned about voltage drop as the wire run is short. These conductors may be connected to larger-gauge wires (within reason); so long as they are rated to carry the load current, no problems should arise.

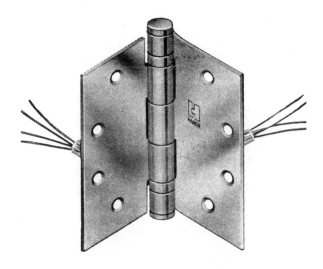

Figure 6–4.   Electric hinge. (Courtesy of Hager Hinge Company)

Electric hinges and pivots are commonly used to conduct power to electric locks, panic bolts, or hold-open devices. They also are used to transmit signals from door-mounted switches and access control devices.

A newer device on the market is shown in Figure 6–6. It is used on doors with standard butt hinges and is designed with larger wire sizes for carrying heavier current loads.

TROUBLESHOOTING

Problems show up infrequently in the wire runs of a system. About the only fault that could occur in the wiring is a break somewhere along the line or too small a conductor for the load being powered or for the length of the run.

If a system has been up and running and problems show up later, they are usually not in the wiring itself. Problems at start-up of a new system could be in the wiring but rarely are.

If a load fails to operate at all at start-up, first check to see if there is power at the source. Next check to see if there is power at the load.

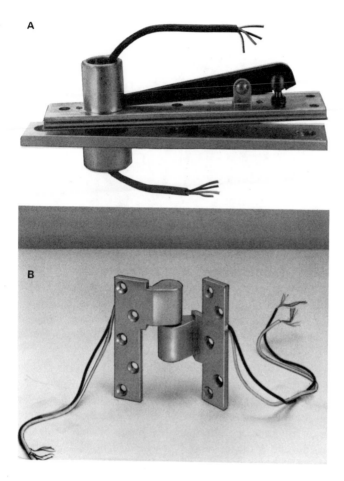

Figure 6–5.   (A) Center-hung electric top pivot and (B) intermediate electric pivot. (Courtesy of Rixson-Firemark, Inc.)

The voltage reading at the load should be within 10 percent of the voltage reading at the source. A lower reading might indicate that the wiring is too small for the distance and is creating an excessive voltage drop. This condition could cause the load to operate inefficiently or not at all. Examples would be dim lights or a sluggish locking device.

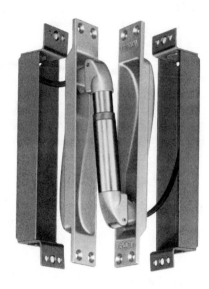

Figure 6–6. Electrical power transfer. It is used in installations with butt hinges and is fully concealed when the door is closed. It is available with two 18 AWG conductors rated for 10 amps at 24VDC (20 amp maximum surge). (Courtesy of Von Duprin)

If there is no voltage at the load, there might simply be an open switch in the line. The worse case would be a break somewhere in the wire run. In any case, if preliminary troubleshooting has not solved the problem, and the wiring is suspect, it would be best to refer the matter to the electricians on the job.

Probably the most common problem with wiring begins with selecting the right size conductor. Although using wire that is too large is not cost-effective, wire that is too small can lead to greater costs later on. Always select wire that has insulation suitable to meet code requirements, is correctly sized for the current draw of the load, and is of sufficient size to prevent excessive voltage drop.

7

Monitoring Devices

Monitoring is an important part of any security system. Various types of monitoring sensors report to monitoring indicators the exact status of a lock or of the door itself. This indication can be at the site of the opening or can be reported to a remote location for central monitoring of a complete system.

Monitoring can become very complex in sophisticated high-security systems. Motion detection, CCTV, printed records, and many other components may be part of a large system. This chapter will deal with only the simple, more common monitoring methods, including monitoring switches for lock and door status signaling and the monitoring devices that provide visual and audible indication for these signals. Learning the basics of monitoring will enable you to understand the philosophy of monitoring and, through experience, add to your skill in designing more intricate systems.

MONITORING SWITCHES

We will discuss two methods of monitoring through the use of switches: switches that report the true status of the lock only and switches that report the status of the door only. As will be seen, monitoring of only one condition or, in some cases, both conditions varies according to system requirements.

In Chapter 3, we discussed various lock monitoring switches. Generally, they are mechanical switches that monitor the position of a bolt, latch, cam, or some mechanical part of the lock. They are used to signal that the lock is in a true locked or unlocked mode. In magnetic locks, a reed switch or solid state device is located inside the coil and frame assembly. It monitors the magnetic field and can signal whether a good bond exists between the magnet and armature.

Monitoring switches do not use power, but they control whatever voltage runs through the circuit to power a monitoring alarm or indicator. The switch contact rating must be checked to see whether it can carry the amount of current required by the monitoring devices. Normally, monitoring devices draw only small amounts of current at low voltages. Most mechanical switches can handle moderate amounts of current. Reed-type magnetic switches usually have more delicate contacts and cannot handle much current. In some cases, reed switches are used to switch a relay that draws low current. Heavier relay contacts are then used to carry the higher current loads. (See Figures 7–1 and 7–2.)

Most locking devices are available with some sort of optional monitoring switch. In some cases, it will be necessary to use these switches for properly controlling the locking system. Doors that are automatically operated sometimes use the signal from these switches to ensure that the operator does not start while the lock is in a secure mode. Other conditions may dictate that lock status monitoring is more desirable than door status monitoring.

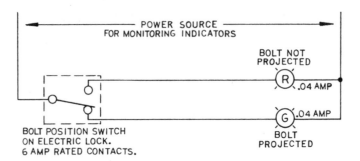

Figure 7–1. The switch contact rating will easily handle a load of one light. The switch is used to control the indicators directly.

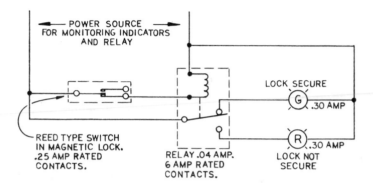

Figure 7–2. The switch contact rating will not handle a load of one light. The switch is used to control lower relay current; higher-rated relay contacts are used to control the indicators.

Lock monitoring switches are normally factory built-in and totally concealed. Consult the lock manufacturer's literature for availability and contact type and rating. Several switch devices monitor the locked or unlocked position of a lock latch or bolt. An example is shown in Figure 7–3. Although these devices are not fully concealed, they offer heavier-duty contacts and are easily mounted into the door frame.

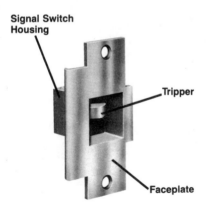

Figure 7–3. Monitor strike for use with mortise or cylindrical locks. (Courtesy of Von Duprin)

They are commonly used with nonelectric mortise and cylindrical locksets to monitor the position of the latchbolt.

The other popular monitoring method is to indicate the open or closed status of a door. A variety of switches are available, but magnetic switches are more popular than mechanical types. Although the mechanical switches have higher contact ratings, the magnetic switches offer better concealment and are less susceptible to tampering. Several types are shown in Figure 7–4.

Mechanical switches are activated by the door pushing against a plunger or roller attached to the switch. They are not as commonly used as magnetic switches in security systems.

Magnetic switches are available in many different configurations. There are switches for wood doors and hollow metal doors, as well as for swinging, sliding, and roll-up doors. Several hinge manufacturers also make what is called a monitoring hinge, shown in Figure 7–5.

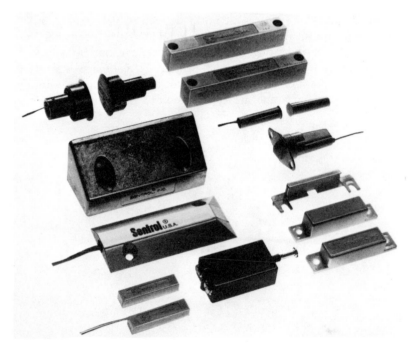

Figure 7–4.   Magnetic contact switches. (Courtesy of Sentrol, Inc.)

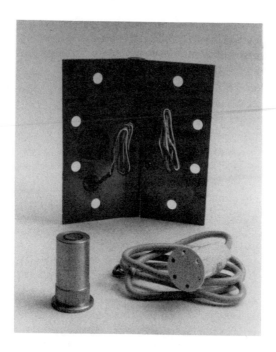

Figure 7–5.   Monitoring hinge components. (Courtesy of McKinney)

This device is totally concealed behind the hinge leaf. Consult the manufacturer's literature for different styles of hinges available with this feature.

A magnetic door switch consists of two parts. One part is the actuating magnet, a permanent magnet mounted in or on a nonferrous housing or bracket. The second part is a small reed switch mounted in a matching housing. The switch contacts are very similar to the switch contacts described in Chapter 5. The lever or swinger of the switch is light enough to be moved by the magnetic field of an actuator magnet when it is moved close to the switch. The gap between the contacts is very small, and little movement is necessary to open and close them. Figure 7–6 is an enlarged sketch of a magnetic reed switch.

The door switch is typically attached to the frame of the door, and the actuating magnet is attached to the door itself. When the door is opened, the magnet moves away from the switch, causing its contacts

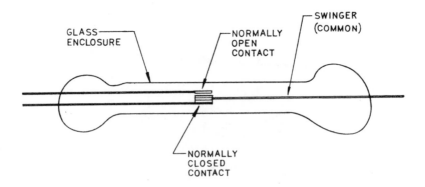

Figure 7–6. Typical glass-enclosed SPDT reed switch (enlarged drawing). The switch would normally have leads attached to contact and swinger ends and would be mounted in a plastic housing.

to change state. It is common practice in the alarm industry to use a normally open switch, which is held closed by the actuating magnet when the door is in the closed position. When the door is opened, the magnet moves away, causing the contacts to return to an open state. The alarm system is wired so that an "open" in the circuit causes the alarm to sound. Magnetic switches are also available with SPDT contacts. This type of switch may be used to monitor both the open and the closed status of the door, as shown in Figure 7–7.

Door monitor switches may be used to sound an alarm or simply to indicate the status of the door. As mentioned in Chapter 3, these switches may also be used to control the locking device itself. Such uses would include keeping electric bolts from projecting while the door is open and initiating locking of other doors in an interlock system.

The switch may also be used to control a multicontact relay, where additional contacts are necessary to signal other equipment in the system. Examples of other equipment that can be coordinated with the opening and closing of doors are CCTV, X-ray machines, fans, and lights. When controlling DC relays, a diode should be added across the relay coil. This will protect the switch contacts from spikes that occur when the current is removed from the relay coil.

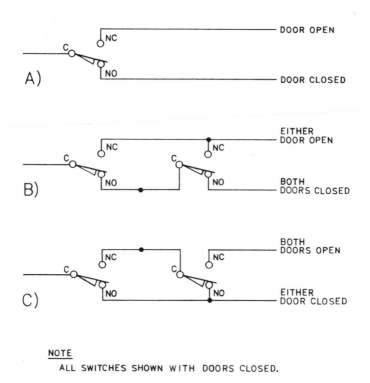

NOTE
ALL SWITCHES SHOWN WITH DOORS CLOSED.

Figure 7–7. Monitoring circuits for single and double doors.

Magnetic switches are available in several contact forms: normally open, normally closed, SPDT with both NC and NO contacts, and DPDT with two sets of contacts. The contact rating generally runs under one amp, and gap distance for actuation is around one-half inch. Wide-gap switches are available, sometimes requiring orientation of the actuating magnet, as they are polarity-sensitive. A good variety of switch and magnet configurations are available, covering many door and frame types. Depending on the type of housing selected, these switches are available with wire or screw terminations.

I must once again caution you always to check the switch contact rating against the load it is to switch. Magnetic switch contacts do not carry much current and are susceptible to having the contacts "welded" together by voltage spikes from inductive loads.

As in previous chapters, I will mention high-security devices only briefly. Several monitoring switches used in high-security and detention systems are readily available from manufacturers that specialize in such systems. More advanced practitioners of electronic security will become involved in these systems. I mention these devices here because a unique situation in an otherwise normal system may require the use of these high-security components.

VISUAL INDICATORS

Without some means of "reading" the signals from a lock or door monitoring device, they would be useless. One such means would be to provide a visual device that the switch could turn on and off. The following devices are used to visually indicate the status or change in status of the lock or door:

1. Indicator lights—color-coded, flashing, or continuous
2. Digital readout
3. Video camera
4. Printer

We will discuss only indicator lights here, as they are the simplest and most economical devices for this purpose. The other items would be used only in more complex systems, and they would require a deeper study than we can provide in this text. Suffice it to say that these items can all be activated by monitoring signals and can provide a great variety of services.

Indicator lights are available in a wide range of sizes, shapes, and mounting methods. Like locking devices, lights are a "load" in the system and are voltage-rated and current-rated. The lights may share the lock power supply or may be powered from a separate power source. If they are powered from a common power source, they must be of the same voltage as the locking device, and their current draw must be included when calculating the size of the power supply.

Generally, the current draw is very small on low-voltage lights. It is also common to find lights rated slightly higher than the system voltage; for example, a light for a 24-volt system might be labeled 28V. This ensures a longer life when the light is operated on 24 volts. Conversely, if a light is operated at too low a voltage, a loss of brightness will occur.

Indicator lights can be obtained in a variety of termination and housing styles. In a security system, they are usually purchased on a mounting plate assembly or even as an option on some locking devices. The common practice of providing the lights on standard-size wall plates allows mounting of the assembly to standard mortise and surface electrical boxes. Some manufacturers offer silk-screened or engraved legends on the plates.

The lights are available in a range of colors; red, green, amber, and white are the most popular. The lamps themselves may be incandescent, neon, or solid state (LED). The incandescent lamp is the most widely used, but there is a distinct trend toward LEDs in recent years. There are several characteristics you may wish to consider when choosing a lamp type.

Incandescents give the maximum light intensity. They are typically available in voltage ranges from 1.5 volts to 28 volts. Because of their construction, they are also the most vulnerable to failure. The filament of the lower-voltage (1.5 to 10 volts) lamps is usually of a more rugged construction. Higher voltages (10 to 28 volts) require a more fragile filament. As power is applied, the filament heats, causing it to become brittle. Excessive voltage, vibrations, or sharp jarring could lead to premature lamp failure. Regulated and filtered power sources help extend the life of incandescent lamps.

Neon lamps are simpler in construction and more economical to use. The great drawback is that they operate on line power and their light output is not as intense. Since you will normally be using low voltages, it is doubtful that you will become involved with neons very often.

The most reliable lights are the solid state light-emitting diodes (LEDs). They are available in voltage ranges from 2 to 28 volts and are very dependable. Although they are not as large or light-intensive as incandescents, design improvements in recent years have led to better light emission. Their high reliability and widespread use in solid state equipment has added to their increasing popularity.

One other style of lighting device you may need to use is large warning lights. These may be used to provide warning of an unsecure or open door over a large area. Almost any large light could be used; a flashing indicator is popular for this purpose.

AUDIBLE INDICATORS

Another way to provide a status signal is by means of audible devices. Unlike lights, which are used to indicate any condition, audibles are usually used to indicate an unlocked or open door status.

The following are the most commonly used audible signals and some of their traditional applications:

1. *Chimes:* A mellow tone suitable for quiet environments. A possible use would be to indicate an opened door in a small store.
2. *Bells:* A general-purpose signal available in a range of sizes. Large bells may be used to signal an alarm condition. Small bells are useful as call signals from a locked door.
3. *Horns:* A blaring sound. Horns can be used to cover a wide area, signaling an unauthorized attempt to breach a secured door.
4. *Sirens:* A shrill, piercing tone used for much the same purpose as a horn. The high irritation level of sirens makes them popular as remote signals on central consoles to initiate a purposeful response.
5. *Buzzers:* A distinct vibrating sound that can range over a wide level of loudness. Buzzers are commonly used for local signaling of an unlocked or open door condition. Buzzers may also be used as call signals.

In security system work, you will most often be using horns, sirens, and buzzers. All of these devices are available in a wide range of sizes and styles. As with indicator lights, some manufacturers provide audible devices on standard-size switch plates for convenience of mounting.

Audible devices are also a "load" in the system and are voltage- and current-rated. The same rules apply as those for indicator lights; the devices may share a common power supply or may have their own. The current draw to be added to a system may vary, however, as power consumption varies with size and type of device.

It is best that audible devices be operated at the voltage for which they are rated. The only exception would be devices that are rated to operate over a designated voltage range. These devices are designed to produce varying levels of sound, depending on whether the input voltage is at the high or low end of the range. This feature is normally found on the siren devices.

Another factor in selecting audibles is the decibel rating, which is a measure of sound pressure level. Decibel (dB) levels change with distance; one notable peculiarity is that to double the loudness at the same distance, you have to add only three decibels.

SELECTING MONITORING DEVICES

Selecting monitoring devices requires a survey of the security system as a whole. Requirements for security, life safety, or just user convenience will dictate which switches, lights, and audibles should be used and their location in the system. I will provide some tips on using each device. Your expertise in selection will grow with your increasing knowledge of what is available and your experience with actual systems.

Monitoring switches are selected to provide a signal for whatever condition you wish to monitor. If you want to know the true physical condition of the door, a door status switch must be used. A common error is the selection of a lock status switch with the belief that a "locked" indication also means "door closed." This is not always true, as a latch or bolt may be projected while the door is open. Moreover, an "unlocked" indication does not necessarily indicate "door open." Be sure to know the precise condition you are trying to indicate.

The diagrams in Figure 7–7 show several methods of indicating door status. A question always arises of whether the status switch can be defeated. Any switch can be defeated if you know its location and the operation it performs within the system. Generally, however, only a professional criminal, with advance knowledge, could defeat a system.

If this possibility is likely, high-security switches can be used, or other switches can be added to back up the system. For example, two door status switches can be used on the same door. If they were wired as shown in Figure 7–7B, both switches would have to be closed to indicate "door closed." This would mean that a person would have to locate and defeat two switches in order to cause an erroneous indication. Another option would be to use a door status switch and lock status switch. As shown in Figure 7–8, two conditions must be met before a "secure" indication can occur.

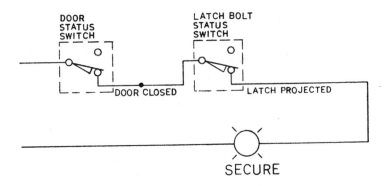

Figure 7–8. Monitoring circuit for true "secure" indication.

The method of mounting must also be considered for door status switches. Surface-mount switches are commonly used in rehab work, but it is best to conceal the switch as much as possible. Ideally, in new construction, the frame would be prepared for flush-mounted switches selected for the system. Several mounting methods for different types of doors are shown in Figure 7–9. When it is necessary to surface mount, try to obtain the switch and actuator in a color that harmonizes with the door and frame color.

I have often been told, "I'll have to use surface switches; the frame is filled with concrete." There is a proper way to use concealed switches, however. It requires extra work, but the result is well worth it.

Selecting visual indicators is usually a simple job. After determining which functions are to be indicated, it is only a matter of selecting a light assembly best suited for your mounting conditions. The most important consideration is that you have the proper signals to control the lights. I have often seen light panels selected with three color-coded lamps but signal provisions to light only two of them.

As shown in Figure 7–7A, the door status switch is capable of controlling two lights—one to indicate "door open" and one to indicate "door closed." Some people would argue that one light is sufficient and that its "off" state would indicate the opposite condition. I would argue, however, that with a two-light system, you could retain status indication even with a burnt-out bulb.

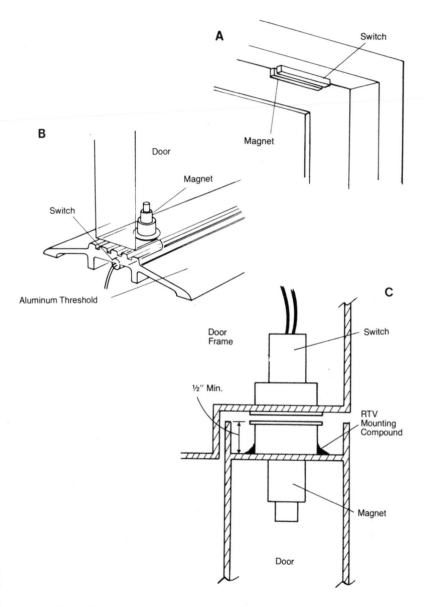

Figure 7–9. Door status switch applications. (A) Surface mount. (B) Threshold mount. (C) Concealed mount. (Courtesy of Sentrol, Inc.)

Selecting colors of lamps or lens covers can precipitate another argument. I have always preferred green for door secure or closed, red for door not secure or open. I have heard good arguments for the opposite, and I hope standardization will be reached someday. Another method of monitoring is possible with a three-light system. The indications might be green for door secure (closed and locked), amber for door not secure (closed and unlocked), and red for door open. This type of monitoring is more likely to be used on central monitoring consoles.

For simple systems, I feel that at least one light—to indicate "door locked"—should be present. The light may be mounted on the lock itself or on a nearby control switch assembly. Its inclusion in the system may prevent unnecessary forcing of a locked door.

The addition of an audible device usually indicates the desire for higher security. Audibles may be used on-site to encourage an intruder to leave or to warn occupants of an unsecure opening. Their use at a central location is to alert a guard to an unsecure condition or a breach of security.

The selection of the proper audible device for an application is governed by the purpose it is to serve. A bell or small buzzer may be used to cover a small, noncritical area—as a call signal or to indicate that a door has been unlocked. Horns are among the more versatile audible devices, since they have a wide range of sound outputs. They can be toned down or made to scream, and they can produce continuous sound or intermittent blasts. A horn's startling sound makes it ideal for large or critical areas, and the rasping sound it produces usually draws immediate response.

Sirens, which are available in steady or pulsating pitches, produce a unique sound. They are commonly used to indicate a violation condition. Buzzers have the lowest decibel ratings and are normally used to call attention rather than to cause alarm.

Consideration must be given to the ambient noise level in the area in which the audible is to be located. The sound produced by the audible should differ from background noise and should override it by at least six decibels. The size of the area to be covered should also be considered in the selection process. A large area may require a loud signal or the use of several small devices.

The mounting of the device can also affect its performance. Horns should be rigidly mounted to ensure that none of their energy is absorbed by the mounting surface. Buzzers mounted on a resonant surface can sound much louder.

You will often need to combine an audio device with visual indicators. Most security product manufacturers offer standard combination assemblies covering simple system requirements.

MONITORING SYSTEMS

As the size of the system and the level of security increases, monitoring takes on new dimensions, and the need for a central monitor, covering an entire system, becomes apparent. Whatever takes place at a door should be reported to a central location, where someone can oversee the condition of each door in the system at a glance. Control of each lock or zone of locks may also be included at the central console.

The term *console* covers a very wide range of equipment available on the market. Some of the other terminology you may see for this type of equipment includes *control console, monitoring console, control panel, monitoring panel, control system, surveillance center;* the list goes on and on. All of these terms describe varying degrees of centrally located equipment that allow a single person to observe and control a security system.

Consoles may range from a one-door system to systems that monitor any number of doors. They may include lights, controls, printers, closed circuit television (CCTV), and alarms. Mounting options include desktop, rack mount, flush wall mount, and surface wall mount. Graphic display panels, which are increasing in popularity, are custom built to the owner's specifications.

The number of options and the great variety of combinations make it impossible to provide an in-depth study of consoles in this text. Figures 7–10 and 7–11 will give you some idea of what is available.

When systems requirements indicate the need for a central console or panel, the following guidelines can help you determine the type of equipment you are looking for. Most of the consoles or control panels you will become involved with will be simple in function. Most often, they will include only monitoring lights or lights and basic controls. Answering the following questions will bring you a long way toward determining just what you are looking for:

Figure 7–10. Desktop console for a small system. (Courtesy of Security Engineering, Inc.)

Figure 7–11. Desktop console for a large system. (Courtesy of Locknetics Security Products)

1. Monitoring only?
   —How many lights per zone?
   —What color(s)?
2. Controls also?
   —What type of switch? (toggle, pushbutton, etc.)
   —What function? (alternate action, momentary)
3. How many zones? (individual doors to be serviced)
4. Any master controls? (console on/off switch, power light, etc.)
5. What other features are desired? (fire panel tie-in, alarm, etc.)
6. What style of mounting?

Once these questions are answered, you could pretty much sketch out the console front panel. If you have access to security products literature, you may even find a standard console that will suit your needs. Another possibility is to send your information to a security products manufacturer. At any rate, I can guarantee that someone has a standard unit that will cover most of your needs or will quote you on a custom unit designed specifically to your requirements.

Once again, I will add a cautionary note: Make sure that your door equipment includes the proper signaling devices to control the console monitoring lights or alarms.

TROUBLESHOOTING

The first step in troubleshooting a monitoring system for suspected faults is to find out whether a problem truly exists. Many times I have been confronted with "The green secure light is burnt out!" or some similar statement. A high percentage of the time, further checking reveals that the lock has been legally turned off or the status switch has not been hooked up.

Most troubleshooting can be done by letting the system diagnose itself. Start by putting everything in its normal condition—door closed, lock switch on, and so forth. Using simple logic and operating the system may uncover the problem immediately. We could not possibly cover every problem that is likely to occur, but several examples should give you an idea of how to progress in troubleshooting.

System
Door with door status switch. Monitoring panel with red "door open" light and green "door closed" light.

Problem: The green light fails to go on.

Solution:
1. Does the red light go on when the door is opened? If so, the green light is most likely bad, and it may be easier to replace it at this point; or proceed to Step 2.
2. With a meter, check for the voltage on the green light with the door closed. If voltage is present, the light is bad.
3. If no voltage appears with the door closed, the light may be good and the door status switch is bad or needs adjustment.
4. If the red light does not go on with the door open, the door status switch is not hooked up, power is not hooked up, or the door status switch needs adjustment.
5. Disconnect the door status switch from the wiring. Check the switch with the meter while opening and closing the door. If the switch works, both lights may be bad. If the switch doesn't work, replace it.

Problem: The green light goes on with the door open; the red light goes on with the door closed.

Solution: The door status switch is wired in reverse. Switch the NC and NO contact wires, either at the door switch or at the monitor panel.

Problem: Both lights are always on.

Solution: Check the door status switch. The contacts may be "welded." Check the current draw of the lights; it may exceed the switch contact rating. Replace the switch. Use a switch with a higher contact rating or change to lights with lower current draw.

For door status switch adjustment, mechanical switches are easy enough to check for proper actuation by the door. Magnetic reed switches are a little more difficult to check. If the switch is not operating the system, use another magnet to actuate it by hand. By observing either a set of monitoring lights or a meter, you can determine whether the switch is working. If the switch works, the actuating magnet is not mounted in the correct position on the door.

Sometimes the gap between the actuating magnet and the switch is too great for actuation to occur. The opposite problem would be actuation occurring too early. This can be due to the location of the switch or, sometimes, to a switch that is too sensitive.

Generally, most problems occur during system hookup and are caused by errors in wiring or incompatible components. Once a system has been properly operating for a while, any problems are usually caused by component failure.

Some installers set up entire systems on the bench before they go out on the job. The time spent doing this could save countless hours ironing out difficulties on the job.

The most important tool you will use in troubleshooting will be the multimeter. Chapter 9 discusses use of the meter for this purpose.

8

Building a System

We have reached the point where we should be able to piece together all we have learned to form a complete security system. In the preceding chapters, we have gained knowledge of each of the components necessary to a security system. Each category includes a variety of components that provide ways to solve most circumstances that will arise in security planning.

Published figures nearly always indicate an increase in crime. Crimes against the person have caused people to feel more insecure than ever before. There has been enormous growth in security systems designed to protect lives and property. Several building codes now specify minimum standards to resist illegal entry. Insurance company emphasis and owner awareness have increased security provisions during the planning stages of new construction. Concern for security has also caused increasing design and sales of security equipment for existing buildings.

There are many approaches to designing a security system, and all involve a thorough knowledge of what equipment is available and what is best for a given situation.

SYSTEM SURVEY AND LAYOUT

There is no single answer to what comprises the best security system. All individuals will design according to their particular knowledge of

159

security products, specifications, installation, and codes. One thing we all will have to do is examine the need, purpose, and funds available for the proposed system.

A survey of the area to be protected should be the first step. This can either be done on-site, for existing structures, or by using blueprints or sketches of a proposed structure. This should be done whether the system is for an entire building, a corridor, or even a single door. The information gathered will make the actual system layout much easier.

Table 8–1 provides general formats for recording survey information. They are offered as guidelines only, but they should give you some idea of the information necessary to design a complete and proper system. The system survey may vary greatly, depending on the type of job to be done. The door survey should include as much information as is available. It will also be necessary to coordinate the security hardware with the builders' hardware on the opening.

The following is a suggested procedure for creating a security system. It is meant as a guideline only, as you will develop your own format and sequence on the basis of your personal preference and the job at hand.

Step 1

First, establish the actual needs of the system. The owner may have a particular system in mind, but it may not always be the best solution to a particular problem. It is up to you to lend your expertise on products, cost-effectiveness, code conformance, and so on, to provide a proper system.

Write up, in detail, what the system is to accomplish. This, in effect, becomes part of the system specification. Once agreed upon, it will establish exactly how the system is to perform after installation. Every system will be different, but the following list should give you a general idea of some system requirements:

Stores: Shoplifters leaving through emergency exits. After-hours control of perimeter doors. Control of stockrooms and delivery areas.

Factories: Employees leaving with equipment and supplies through exit doors. Stockroom and computer room control. Entrance by unauthorized persons.

Table 8-1. Sample Survey Sheets

SYSTEM SURVEY	JOB NAME:
Type of Facility:	(hospital, bank, jewelry store, etc.)
New Construction?	Existing?
Total Openings:	Single:	Pair:	Double Egress:
Standby Power Required?	Fire Panel Tie-In Required?
Central Console Required?	Monitoring:	Control:
Notes:	

DOOR SURVEY	DOOR NUMBER(S):
Door & Frame Material:	Size:
Single:	Pair:	Double Egress:	Hand of Door:
In-swinging:	Out-swinging:	Sliding:	Other:
Interior:	Exterior:	Fire-Labeled:	Designated Egress:
Manual:	Automatic:
Type of Locking Device:	Surface Mount:	Mortise:
Outside Control (on-site):	Type:	Monitoring:
Inside Control (on-site):	Type:	Monitoring:
Delay Egress:	Delay Relocking:
Interlock:	Describe:
Standby Power:	
Notes:	

161

Entertainment Centers: Entrance through nondesignated doors to gain free admission. Control of emergency exits through fire or hazard panels.

Institutions: Unauthorized egress by patients. Control of drug rehab and detention areas. Control of drug and arms rooms.

Government Facilities: Control of unauthorized entrance to cause destruction or bodily harm. Unauthorized egress to steal documents and equipment.

Airports: Control of restricted areas. Unauthorized use of emergency exits.

Of course, you could simply lock all the doors, but security would then conflict with life safety. Code requirements and the balance between security and life safety are discussed later in this chapter. Suffice it to say, here, that when you are establishing the needs of the system, you must provide for all the needs of the openings in question. You may have to come back and finish or modify this step after finishing the next step.

Step 2

After you have determined the size and desired functions of the system, I recommend that you prepare a door-by-door layout of the items required. Figure 8–1 represents a single-door layout. If this were the only door in the system, a separate survey sheet might not be necessary. The operation description (in the figure caption) covers just about all you need to know at this point. In this layout, I have itemized only the electronic security hardware. This list could include or should be coordinated with a list of the builders' hardware that is also needed, including the bored lockset, a door closer, hinges, and so on.

The layout shown in Figure 8–1 includes electronic items necessary to the system. Placement of the items on the sketch may not represent their true location but can serve as a guideline. Any other available information should be added to the drawing. Unless a formal presentation is to be made, a hand sketch is adequate.

Step 3

A riser diagram and point-to-point hookup diagram will eventually be needed. These drawings may not be the responsibility of the person

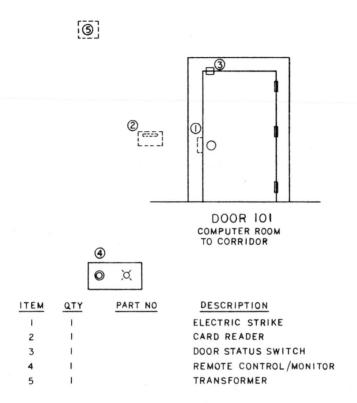

ITEM	QTY	PART NO	DESCRIPTION
1	1		ELECTRIC STRIKE
2	1		CARD READER
3	1		DOOR STATUS SWITCH
4	1		REMOTE CONTROL/MONITOR
5	1		TRANSFORMER

Figure 8–1. Single-door layout with electronic security hardware. Operation: The door is normally locked by a standard exit function bored lockset. Access is by an electric strike activated by an outside card reader; egress is by an inside knob. The interior control panel allows maintained unlocking by pushbutton. The panel indicator light (red) monitors door-open condition. A transformer powers the indicator and strike.

who is doing the system survey and layout. They may be done by an architect's electrical engineer or an electrical contractor, or they may even be supplied by the electronic hardware manufacturer or distributor. The riser diagram shows the number of conductors to be run from the various components. It may also include the wire size if the person making the drawing is qualified to calculate the wire sizes required. (At the time of this drawing, the lengths of the wire runs may not be known). This drawing is primarily used by the electrical people who are "pulling" the wire for the system. The hookup diagram shows where to connect each wire to the system components. It may also be called a system schematic. It is sometimes easier to make this drawing first and do the riser diagram later. At this time, it would be a good practical exercise to try to generate the hookup diagram for Figure 8–1. You may find it easiest to create a system schematic first. Depending on the method you choose, your final sketches should be similar to those shown in Figures 8–2, 8–3, and 8–4. Although the general locations of the components may vary, the electrical paths should be the same.

Step 4

For this system, I chose to sketch a system schematic first (see Figure 8–2). The schematic is usually needed to identify all the contacts necessary to provide proper operation of the components being powered. It provides a "map" of the flow of power and is usually indispensable in troubleshooting, especially in larger systems. On this type of

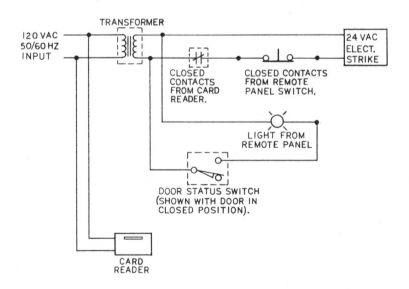

Figure 8–2.   Schematic of a single-door system.

drawing, the physical location of components is totally irrelevant; the idea is to get the system to work electrically. As a simple starting point, I recommend drawing the power lines directly to all components that need power. You can than start adding along the lines the proper contacts necessary to "make" or "break" the power circuit. You may end up discarding several sketches before you hit a good layout. This is typical; with practice, you will find it easier to do and will look forward to the challenge of more complex systems.

The schematic in Figure 8–2 shows the actual electrical operation of the system. The components are located so as to provide an easy-to-follow drawing. Trying to show components in their actual physical relationship usually results in a drawing that is difficult to read, with many crossover lines. This drawing becomes useful in planning the riser diagram and for later troubleshooting of the system.

Step 5

It is sometimes a toss-up whether to draw a riser diagram or a hookup diagram first. Systems can vary; sometimes they are simple enough that one "combination" drawing can provide all the information necessary.

If you try a riser diagram for this system first, you might end up with a mess of wires running from each component in all directions. The purpose of the riser diagram is to provide the most practical method of routing the wire for the system. Often, it is better to let the electrical people involved with the job generate this drawing from your schematic or hookup diagram. For this system, I thought it would be easiest to provide one common place for all the wire connections to be made. Providing a junction box in the system allows the wires from each component to be run to one location, which also provides one single point to do all troubleshooting.

Figure 8–3A shows the wiring for each item drawn in the schematic running to a junction box. By following the paths of the conductors in the schematic, the hookup drawing can be completed, as shown in Figure 8–3B. As can be seen, five wire nut terminations could tie this entire system together. In larger, more complex systems, the junction box might contain hundreds of numbered terminals. The point-to-point wiring diagram for such a system would be a simple list of which wire goes to each numbered terminal. Each wire would be coded by a color, letter, or number.

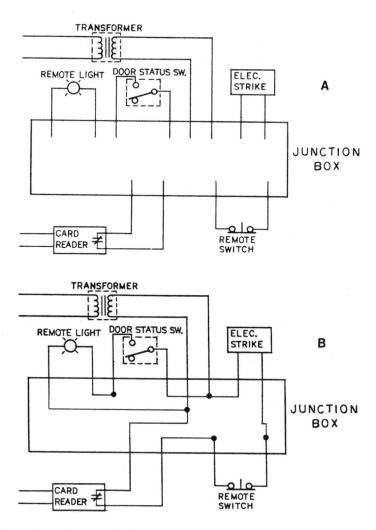

Figure 8–3. Point-to-point wiring diagram of a single-door system using a common junction box. The drawing should also include the colors of the wires for each item. (A) Incomplete wiring to junction box. (B) Complete wiring to junction box.

Step 6

The riser diagram can now be completed, as shown in Figure 8–4. This drawing may be nothing more than a copy of the door layout, as shown in Figure 8–1, with the wire runs penciled in. Note the addition of a junction box to the diagram and hardware list. This allows the wire runs to become simple, direct routes. The riser diagram is usually a separate document for whoever is pulling the wire for the system.

As mentioned earlier, a single person may not be responsible for all of these drawings. The formats of the drawings and wire lists also may vary greatly from job to job. The drawings in this section are provided

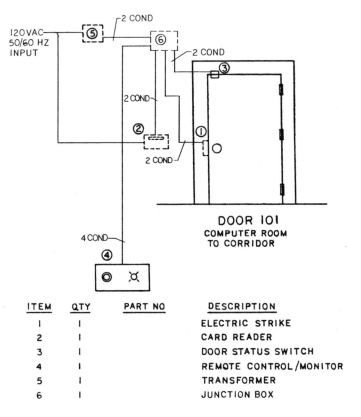

ITEM	QTY	PART NO	DESCRIPTION
1	1		ELECTRIC STRIKE
2	1		CARD READER
3	1		DOOR STATUS SWITCH
4	1		REMOTE CONTROL/MONITOR
5	1		TRANSFORMER
6	1		JUNCTION BOX

Figure 8–4. Riser diagram for a single-door system.

only to show the concept and thought process involved in documenting system wiring information.

SIMPLE LOCKING SYSTEMS

In this section, I will provide several layouts for simple locking systems. The variations of systems are endless, but the simple systems shown will give you a basic building block for more complex systems. In each case, it should be understood that the components are selected to suit the conditions of an actual situation. In all of the layouts, the system voltage values have been omitted, as they can vary. In nearly all cases, the systems will be 12 or 24 volts.

Figure 8–5 is intended only to illustrate the use of the transformer, rectifier, and DC power supply. As shown in Figures 8–5A and 8–5B, a lock rated for AC operation needs only a transformer as a power source. Figures 8–5C and 8–5D show a DC lock, which needs the addition of a rectifier to change AC to DC before power enters the lock. The rectifier can be located at the transformer or at the lock. An alternative method for powering DC locks is to provide a DC power supply, as shown in Figures 8–5E and 8–5F. Other diagrams provided in this section will show circuits for specific types of locks.

The three diagrams in Figure 8–6 show simple electric strike circuits. As shown in Figure 8–6A the transformer (T1) supplies AC to the strike when the normally open switch (S1) is closed. The strike releases with a buzzing sound, which acts as an "open" signal.

In Figure 8–6B, the transformer (T1) supplies AC to the rectifier (RB1), which converts it to DC. When the normally open switch (S1) is closed, the DC power releases strike silently. The rectifier may be wired to T1 secondary or to strike leads, as shown.

In Figure 8–6C, the fail-safe operation requires that DC be continuously supplied to the strike through the normally closed switch (S1). If the rectifier (RB1) were not used, the strike would buzz constantly during the locked cycle. Opening the switch contact releases the strike by interrupting power.

Figure 8–7 shows diagrams for fail-safe and fail-secure solenoid-operated bolts. In Figure 8–7A, fail-safe operation requires that all switches be closed before the transformer (T1) supplies power to energize the solenoid and project the bolt. A door status switch (DSS1) is used to ensure that power will not flow to the solenoid unless the door is closed. This switch keeps the bolt from projecting while the door is open; it is sometimes called the automatic relock switch. Note that closed switches are wired in series.

In Figure 8–7B, the fail-secure bolt is normally projected without power. The closing switch (S1) allows the transformer (T1) to supply power to the solenoid, retracting the bolt. When the door is opened, the door status switch (DSS1) closes, keeping power on the solenoid, even if the control switch (S1) is reopened. This switch ensures that the bolt will not project while the door is open. Note that open switches are wired in parallel.

Many solenoid-operated bolts are available with built-in rectifiers and are operated from AC or DC. If a rectifier is required separately, it may be wired as shown in Figure 8–6.

Electromagnets are inherently DC-operated fail-safe devices. They are commonly operated by DC power supplies. They may be operated by AC power only when a rectifier (RB1) is provided, as shown in Figure 8–8A. Available only as fail-safe, they must be controlled by closed contacts (S1).

Electromagnets exhibit a voltage kickback (voltage spike) when they are turned off. If it is not suppressed at the magnet, this spike can damage solid state switching devices in the circuit. Heavier switching contacts can withstand the spike but will have a reduced life span under high usage. Some units are available with built-in suppression devices. If they do not have this feature, two methods of suppression can be added, as shown in Figures 8–8B and 8–8C.

As shown in Figure 8–8B, a metal oxide varistor (MOV) will suppress the voltage spike without polarizing the lock. For reference, a 12-volt unit may use a G.E. Part No. V18ZA3 (clamp voltage = 39) or a 24-volt unit may use a G.E. V27ZA4 (clamp voltage = 53).

As shown in Figure 8–8C, a diode will suppress the voltage spike but will polarize the lock. Care must be taken in hooking up the unit to the power source. A general-purpose diode rated at least 3 amp may be used. The diode must be oriented as shown in the figure (band end toward +).

Note that if a rectifier bridge is provided directly at the magnet, it will suppress any voltage spike. Additional spike suppression devices are not necessary for this condition.

Many discussions have evolved around the placement of suppression devices and control switches for electromagnets. These discourses

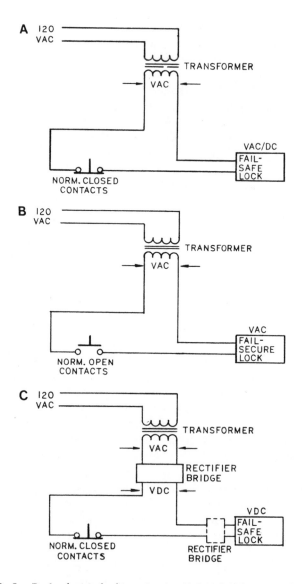

Figure 8–5. Basic electric locking circuits (AC and DC). (A) Fail-safe lock circuit (VAC). (B) Fail-secure lock circuit (VAC). (C) Fail-safe lock circuit (VDC). (D) Fail-secure lock circuit (VDC). (E) Fail-safe lock circuit (VDC). (F) Fail-secure lock circuit (VDC).

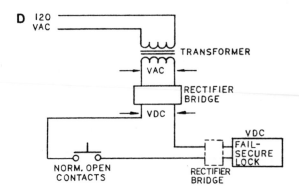

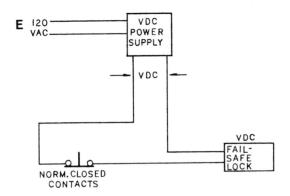

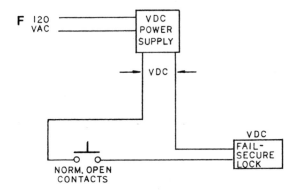

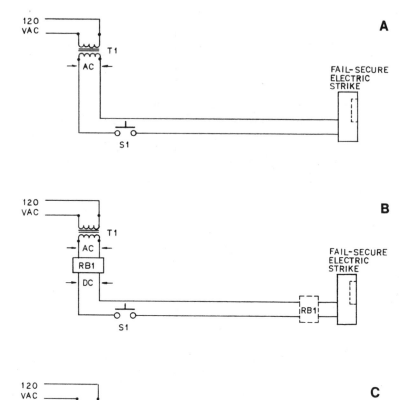

Figure 8–6. Electric strike systems. (A) Fail-secure audible (AC) operation. (B) Fail-secure silent (DC) operation. (C) Fail-safe silent (DC) operation.

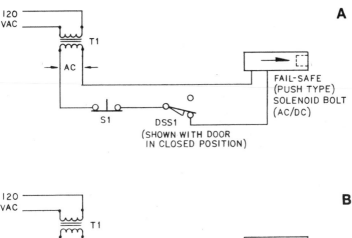

Figure 8–7.   Solenoid-operated bolt systems. (A) Push type. (B) Pull type.

relate to the speed at which an electromagnet will release. It is my opinion that, in most cases, the slight delay (under a half-second) is of no great consequence. About the only occasion it would be beneficial to have the fastest possible release time is when the lock is being released by a switch in a panic device or a simultaneous signal is being sent to an automatic door operator. Figure 8–9 shows wiring diagrams for two methods of control placement. In Figure 8–9A, although the switch contacts are protected from voltage spike by the rectifier (RB1), their placement on the AC side causes a slight time delay in lock release. In Figure 8–9B, switch placement on the DC side results in faster lock release. A suppression device (MOV) may be added to protect the contacts from deterioration due to voltage spike.

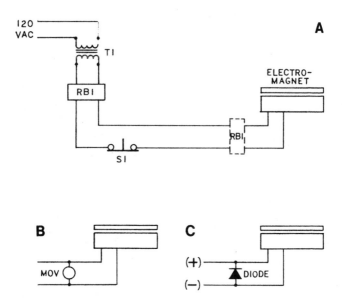

Figure 8–8. Electromagnet systems. (A) With rectifier. (B) With a metal oxide varistor (MOV). (C) With a diode.

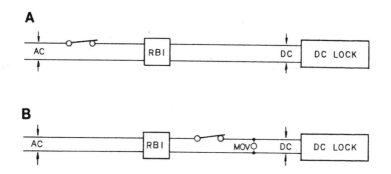

Figure 8–9. Control placement in an electric locking circuit. (A) With switch placement on the AC side. (B) With switch placement on the DC side.

Wiring multiple locks in a system can be done by a variety of methods. Several basic arrangements are shown in Figure 8–10. Figure 8–10A shows multiple locks wired in parallel. The normally closed switch turns the power off to release all fail-safe locks simultaneously. A normally open switch could be used to turn the power on to release all fail-secure locks simultaneously.

Figure 8–10B shows multiple fail-safe locks with a normally closed switch at each lock to provide individual control. The master release switch could be a closed contact from a fire panel.

As shown in Figure 8–10C, multiple fail-secure locks require a normally open switch at each lock for individual control. Since locks require power to initiate release, a master release would require multiple contacts to shunt out each individual control contact.

Wiring switch contacts in a system is usually a very simple procedure that seems to confuse a great many people. Figure 8–11 shows three of the most commonly used methods of wiring contacts for simple control systems. Naturally, many other wiring designs are used to create more complex systems.

As shown in Figure 8–11A, normally closed contacts are generally wired in *series*. An example would be multiple switches to control a fail-safe lock. Opening any contact interrupts the power. As many contacts as desired may be used in a circuit.

As shown in Figure 8–11B, normally open contacts are generally wired in *parallel*. An example would be multiple switches to control a fail-secure lock. Closing any contact completes the power circuit. As many contacts as desired may be used in a circuit.

As shown in Figure 8–11C, it is occasionally desirable to be able to turn a device off or on at one location and to switch it back off or on at another location. Wiring two SPDT contacts (maintained switch) as shown will provide this switching mode.

INTERLOCKING SYSTEMS

Interlocking systems can consist of any number of doors and a great variety of operating modes. Several of the most basic systems can be designed by the correct wiring of simple control switches. This section will present several of these systems and their operating descriptions. More complex systems may require additional electronics, such as multipole relays.

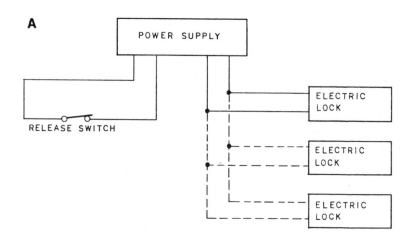

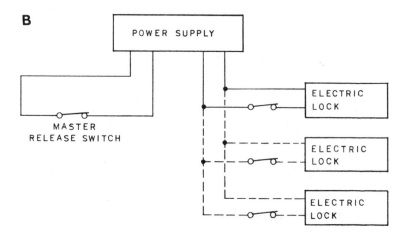

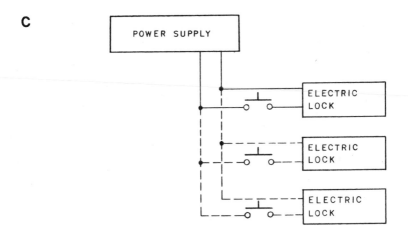

Figure 8–10. Multiple-lock systems. (A) Multiple locks wired in parallel. (B) Multiple fail-safe locks. (C) Multiple fail-secure locks.

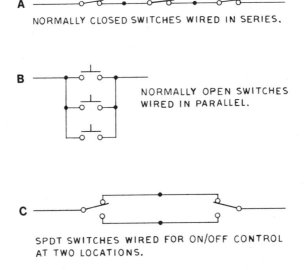

Figure 8–11. Contact wiring arrangements. (A) Normally closed switches wired in series. (B) Normally open switches wired in parallel. (C) SPDT switches wired for on/off control at two locations.

All of the systems presented in this section use door status switches to perform the basic logic required to operate the interlock. It is important that these switches be selected to carry the current required by the locking device(s), as they usually have the most fragile contacts of all the switches in the system. For this reason, only two door systems are diagrammed. Most of the systems could be expanded to have more doors, but a single-door status switch would then have to carry the load of several locks simultaneously. These cases would be better served by using relay logic design.

For each figure, I have provided a brief specification and operation description for the type of system diagrammed.

Communicating Bathroom System (Figure 8–12)

Specification
This is a fail-safe electric locking system to provide privacy and convenience to the occupants of a common bathroom between two rooms. Both doors must be closed to be locked. An emergency release switch or power failure releases both doors. Common usage would be in hospitals, nursing homes, and dormitories.

Operation
Both doors are normally closed and unlocked. The occupant enters the bathroom and operates the master switch to lock both doors. Both doors must be closed to initiate locking. An emergency release switch outside each door will unlock both doors. An associated light indicates when both doors are in locked condition.

Mantrap (Figure 8–13)

Specification
This is a fail-safe electrical locking system to provide restricted and highly controlled access to a specific area. The mantrap system controls access by the use of two doors, which cannot be opened at the same time, in a pass-through area. The system allows "trapping" of a person within the pass-through area until identification is made. Common usage would be for entrances to jewelry stores, money-counting rooms, and high-security areas.

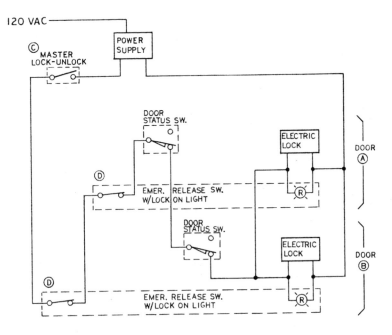

Figure 8–12. Electric locking circuit for a communicating bathroom.

Operation

Both doors are normally closed and locked. Entrance door (A) can be unlocked by an authorized person using a key switch, card reader or other restricted device. This device may be replaced by a call station, requiring an inside guard to release the door. Once in the mantrap, the person must call for identification, which may be by a closed-circuit TV camera installed inside the trap. The inside guard may then release

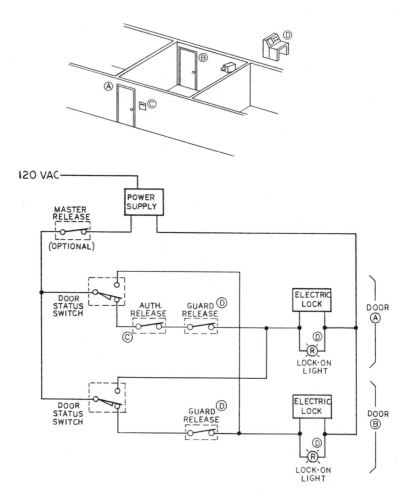

Figure 8–13. Electric locking circuit with a mantrap.

the second door (B), and the person can pass into the restricted area. If identification is not made, the guard may leave the person secured in the trap until further action is taken. The door status switches provide an override of any release switch, so that no door can be unlocked if the other door is open. The master release switch is optional and will release any locked door, such as a fire panel tie-in.

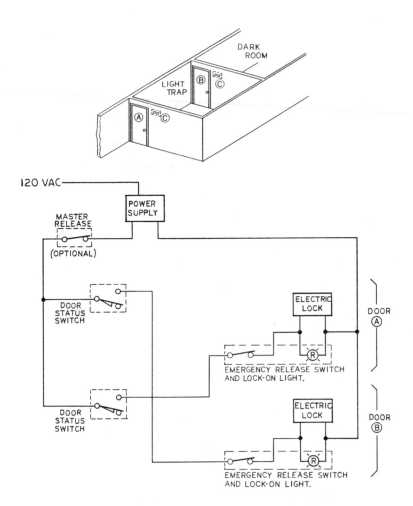

Figure 8–14. Electric locking circuit with a two-door safety interlock.

Two-Door Safety Interlock (Figure 8–14)

Specification

This is a fail-safe electric locking system to prevent opening of more than one door at a time. It provides emergency release switches in areas with no other means of egress. Common usage would be to control or restrict the flow of light, air, or people in darkrooms, clean rooms, or similar areas in hospitals, laboratories, and industrial and military facilities.

Operation

Both doors are normally closed and unlocked. Opening one door automatically locks the other door, which remains locked until the open door is closed. Emergency release switches may be provided in areas where personnel could be trapped if a door were left ajar. The master release switch is optional and will release any locked door, such as a fire panel tie-in.

Two-Door Security Interlock (Figure 8–15)

Specification

This is a fail-safe electric locking system to prevent opening of more than one door at a time. Devices for authorized unlocking may be provided on both sides of each door if required. Common usage would be in restricted rooms, such as money-counting rooms and drug storage rooms, where there is no supervisor or guard control station. For higher security, lock status switches may be included to override release switches (see Figure 8–16).

Operation

Both doors are normally closed and locked. Unlocking and opening one door overrides the release switch for the other door. The second door cannot be unlocked until the first door is closed. The master release switch is optional and will release any locked door, such as a fire panel tie-in.

Two-Door Security Interlock with Added Security (Figure 8–16)

Specification and operation of this interlock are identical to those for Figure 8–15, except for the addition of the lock status switch. This switch rather than the door status switch, now controls the interlock, increasing security. In the prior circuit, the door had to be unlocked and *opened* before interlocking would occur. In this circuit, *unlocking* a door immediately voids the release for the other door.

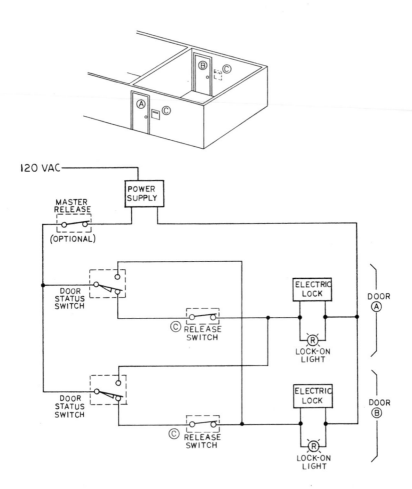

Figure 8–15.   Electric locking circuit with a two-door security interlock.

Two-Door Safety/Security Interlock (Figure 8–17)

Specification
This is a fail-safe electric locking system to prevent opening of more than one door at a time. This system is a variation of the systems shown in Figures 8–13 through 8–16 and could be used in any of

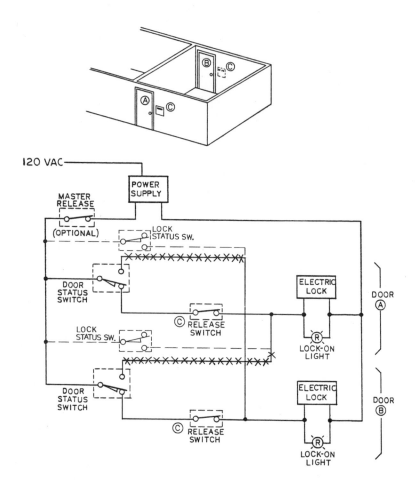

Figure 8–16.   Electric locking circuit with a two-door security interlock with added security.

those situations. Where the other systems specify both doors normally locked or both normally unlocked, this system provides one normally unlocked door and one normally locked door.

Operation
Both doors are normally closed. Door (A) is normally unlocked; door (B) is normally locked. Opening door (A) overrides the release switch

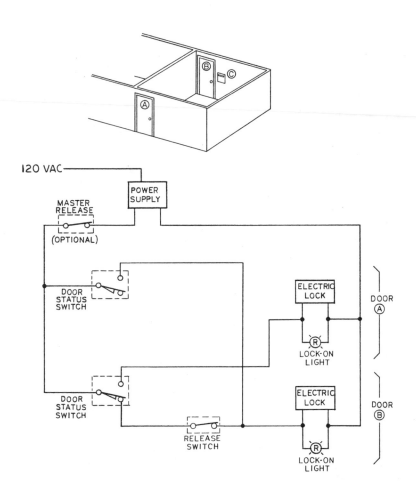

Figure 8–17.   Electric locking circuit with a two-door safety/security inter-lock.

for door (B) until door (A) is closed again. Unlocking and opening door (B) will cause door (A) to lock until door (B) is closed again.

SPECIAL SYSTEMS

"Special" systems may include anything a person can dream up; they may be unique, one-time-only designs for a specific situation. With electronics, all things are possible; no job need be turned down, provided that enough time and money are available to design and build the system.

Several situations show up more and more frequently, and I have selected four of the most common systems for these situations to present in this section. To avoid redundancy, I will show all systems using fail-safe locking devices. Several of these systems could use fail-secure locking devices by changing the control contacts to normally open, as described earlier in this chapter.

Automatic Time Switch Control (Figure 8–18)

Specification
This is a fail-safe electric locking system to be controlled automatically for day/night locking cycles.

Operation
The lock release switch is used to release the lock manually whenever it is in a locked state. Additional control is provided by contacts from the time switch. The time switch is programmed to open and close the contacts during certain hours of a 24-hour period. For example, this could automatically provide an unlocked condition during working hours and a locked condition after working hours. Timers are avail-

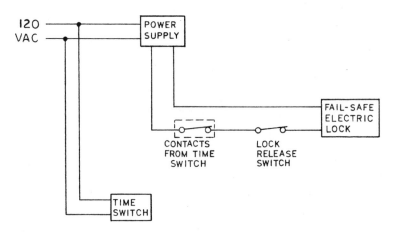

Figure 8–18. Electric locking circuit with an automatic time switch control.

able with skip-a-day features to exclude the unlocking cycle during weekends.

Note that the timer shown would have to be reset after a power outage. Although they are more expensive, there are time switches available with DC-operated motors. They could be operated by a DC power supply with standby battery power. The DC power supply could also power the locking device.

Equipment Interlock (Figure 8–19)

Specification
This is a fail-safe electric locking system to provide control over an X-ray machine that is never to be turned on if the door is in an unlocked condition.

Operation
The lock release switch is shown closed, causing the lock to energize. The lock monitor switch closes, completing the circuit to the relay coil. Energizing the relay causes its normally open contact to close. The equipment control switch can now be used to turn the equipment on.

If the lock release switch were opened, the lock would release. The lock monitor switch would open, causing the relay to "drop out." Its held-closed contacts would fall open, breaking the circuit to the equipment. Closing the equipment control switch would not turn the equipment on, as the circuit is broken by the open relay contact.

Automatic Door Operator (Figure 8–20)

Specification
This is a fail-safe electric locking system to provide control over an automatic door that is never to be operated if the door is in a locked condition.

Operation
The normally closed relay contact and the closed day/night switch keep the lock energized. The normally open contact of the second contact set of the relay and the open lock monitor switch keep the power circuit to the automatic door operator open.

Closing the floor mat switch energizes the relay, opens the circuit to the lock, and closes the circuit to the door operator. The lock monitor

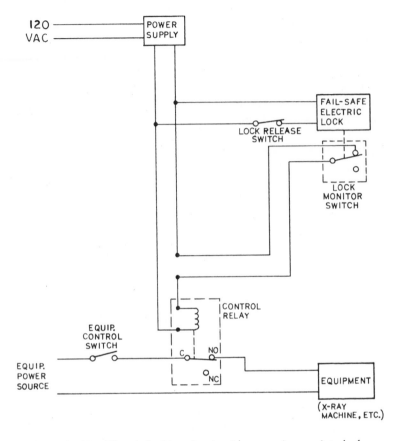

Figure 8–19. Electric locking circuit with an equipment interlock.

switch also closes, completing the circuit to the door operator, allowing the door to open.

If the day/night switch were left open, the lock monitor switch would remain closed. Closing the floor mat switch would still allow the second contact set of the relay to operate the door.

The circuit shown is one basic method of wiring this type of system. Other variations are possible, depending on the desired operation of the system.

It should be noted that the relays added to the circuits in Figures 8–19 and 8–20 would be selected for the same voltage rating as the power supply output. If necessary, they could be selected with a differ-

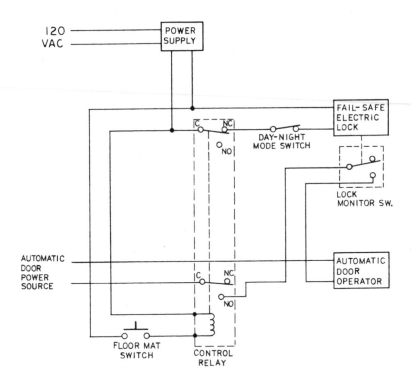

Figure 8–20. Electric locking circuit with an automatic door operator.

ent operating voltage and run from a separate power source. In some cases, the relay may already exist as part of the equipment to be controlled.

Delayed-Egress Control (Figure 8–21)

The system shown in Figure 8–21 is normally wired to a special controller or to a power supply that includes special control logic. This type of system is available from several manufacturers and is becoming increasingly popular.

Until 1981, emergency exit doors could be locked only by means of a latching exit device. Often, they would include an alarm device that would sound whenever the exit device was operated to egress through the opening. Although this provided ample life safety, it offered very little security, as immediate egress was always possible. In many cases,

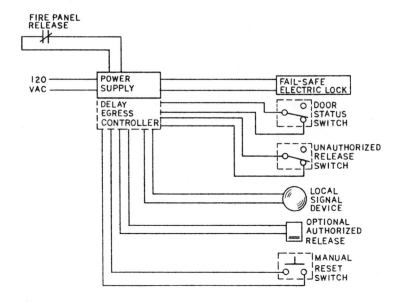

Figure 8–21. Electric locking circuit with a delayed-egress control.

it was not unusual to find exit devices illegally chained and padlocked during certain times of the day.

In 1981, NFPA 101—Life Safety Code was changed to provide more security, without compromising life safety, on openings of this type. The code change allowed for a fifteen-second delayed release of a fail-safe locking device. The outline in Figure 8–21 shows the basic wiring of this type of system. The NFPA 101 section entitled "Special Locking Arrangements" should be consulted for details of this system, as several restrictions apply when using delayed-egress locking.

Specification

This is a fail-safe electric locking system to provide security at a perimeter exit door. Delayed unlocking through use of an exit device is provided to discourage theft, unauthorized entry, and so forth. The system is to be tied to an alarm system to provide immediate release during a fire or other hazard emergency. All components and operation must conform to the NFPA 101 section entitled "Special Egress Arrangements."

Operation

With the door closed and locked, an attempt to egress by operating the exit device causes the release switch in the exit device to signal the controller. The signal device at the door will sound immediately, and the time-delay signal to release the lock will start. At the end of fifteen seconds, the lock will release and the door may be opened. The system will reset by a signal from a manual reset switch to the controller when the door is opened and reclosed.

Immediate release is provided by the tie-in to the fire alarm system. An optional legal release may be included for immediate release of the lock by authorized personnel.

SECURITY AND LIFE SAFETY

In the process of designing an electric locking system, several factors concerning security versus life safety must be considered. In normal situations, the primary concern throughout the design process should be life safety. Life safety and security requirements often create a conflict, especially regarding emergency exit doors. It is in this area that a properly designed electric locking system can provide some degree of compatibility.

The majority of the systems you will encounter will involve areas of protection against theft, destruction of property, and confinement of people. The purpose of the system will therefore be to prevent unauthorized access/egress and to control and limit traffic effectively in designated areas.

The previously described attributes of electric locking certainly provide a great variety of methods by which to solve clients' security needs in a system; but as we have seen, they can also provide a good degree of life safety. For example, the system shown in Figure 8–21 allows cooperation between security interests and life safety interests. Changes in the NFPA Life Safety Code allow some compatibility between security and life safety considerations within a system. Before the code change, fire safety codes required that emergency exit doors in commercial and public buildings remain unlocked as a means of egress in an emergency. This led to the use of these doors for other than emergency egress and seriously reduced the security of the opening.

Alarming the door offered some relief in discouraging unauthorized use of the opening but did little to stop someone who was intent on egressing, especially in unsupervised areas. This led to the illegal use of deadbolts, chains, and other devices, which certainly enhanced security but only by sacrificing life safety. Several fatal fires between late 1979 and 1980 prompted the code change, providing a viable solution to this very common problem.

It is up to you to become familiar with local and national codes so that you will be able to offer the best possible solution to a given problem. Fail-safe electric locks can provide several acceptable methods of securing an opening and providing life safety during an emergency condition. Since the defining characteristic of fail-safe devices is that they fail and become unsecure when power is interrupted, it is possible to secure an opening while still providing a means of egress during an emergency. Methods of releasing the locking device may include local pull stations, central alarm tie-in, or central console control.

In many cases, fire codes may require that there be latching panic hardware on the door. The electric lock may be released by a switch in the panic device—a feature being offered by several manufacturers.

In any system, local approvals may be necessary, and adherence to local, state, and national codes is necessary. Some of the national codes regarding doors, frames, and hardware are noted in Appendix A, but you should remember that local acceptance will be a factor in any system design.

Sometimes, economic factors will affect the quality of a system. Often, life safety features may be looked upon as unnecessary and elaborate add-ons. There may be times that you should avoid jobs that may lead to liability on your part because of some necessary feature the end user refuses to accept. Moreover, a system may be enhanced by the addition of certain features that could be beneficial not only to the salesman but also in reducing the liability of the building owner.

Acceptance of electric security products for solving many security and life safety problems is growing rapidly throughout the world. The increased use of these products in institutions, hospitals, and schools depends, in part, on informing approval authorities of the benefits and legality of the products and system designs. The education of all those involved with electronic security is necessary for dissemination of this information and is, indeed, the prime reason for this book.

9

Troubleshooting

Throughout the preceding chapters, we have discussed troubleshooting for many of the electronic hardware components we have studied. In this chapter, you will learn about one of the most important tools you can possess for troubleshooting electronic components and systems.

First, I will provide some brief notes on necessary safeguards when working with electrical circuits.

SAFETY FIRST

Most electric security equipment operates at low voltages (under 30 volts), and current draws are usually in a low range. Although low-voltage systems are generally considered safe to work with, you should always be aware that line power voltages may be present somewhere in the system. Line power should be isolated from the low-voltage system through an isolation transformer. Line power voltages can be deadly and should not come in contact with your hands, body, or tools.

Always be sure that the power is off when you are doing any work within a circuit. It isn't always high voltage that causes fatal shocks; the effect of a shock is determined by the amount of current flowing through your body.

A current of one-thousandth of an amp (one milliamp) is barely perceptible. Up to 8 milliamps can cause mild to strong surprise. An 8 to 15 milliamp current is unpleasant, but you can usually let go of the item causing the shock. A current over 15 milliamps can lead to "muscular freeze," which can prevent you from releasing whatever you are holding. Currents over 75 milliamps can be fatal.

Of course, several factors determine the danger of electrical shock. The higher the voltage of the power source, the more milliamps would flow through your body. Also, if the power source can produce high current, fatal shock can be caused well below 120 volts.

As examples of high-voltage, low-current shocks, consider your home and your auto. If you walk on dry carpeting in your home in the winter when the humidity is low, you pick up a static charge. If you then touch a grounded object, you feel only a mild shock because the current is so small. The coil of a running auto engine can produce at least 20,000 volts but a very low current. Touching the coil or spark plugs will give you a surprising, but nonfatal shock.

To further reduce the chance of electrical shock, you should stand on a dry, nonconductive surface. If you contact 120-volt line power in this condition, you would feel little shock. If you were standing on a damp basement floor in your bare feet, however, you would feel severe shock. If you were standing in water, you would be electrocuted. Never stand in water, or on a wet surface, when working with electricity!

Working safely requires care, an understanding of what you are doing, and a knowledge of exactly how you will do it. Plan the job in advance, and keep loose items out of the work area. Do not defeat the purpose of protective devices, such as fuses and circuit breakers, by shorting them out or by using higher-rated devices than what is specified. Exercising good judgment and care will protect you and the equipment you are working with.

MULTIMETERS

If any one item can save you time and money in the field, it is the multimeter. It can save you many hours in troubleshooting and quite often can save the cost of obtaining unnecessary consultation.

This instrument, an electronic technician's constant companion, can localize problems in a system. Anyone involved in electronic security systems should have one and should learn the basics of its operation. Once you have learned to work with a multimeter, many of you will also recognize its potential for use in your home and garage.

Two types of meters in use today are the analogue meter (VOM) and the digital meter (DMM). The analogue meter has a pointer that indicates the reading on a calibrated face plate. The digital meter indicates the reading by displaying the actual measurement in numerical form. Digital meters, though more costly than analogue meters, are becoming more popular. The additional cost can be justified by their greater versatility; they are more accurate and reading errors are greatly reduced.

The multimeter is a combination of an ammeter, voltmeter, and ohmmeter in one unit. Its purpose is to make voltage, current, and resistance measurements of components and circuits in an electrical system, and it is designed to provide various ranges for these measurements. A labeled panel and selector switch is provided for selecting various functions and ranges. Two types of meters are shown in Figure 9–1.

The best way to learn how to use your meter is to read the operator's manual for your particular meter and practice a little. The manual is important because different makes of meters vary in both appearance and operating functions.

Select your meter on the basis of your personal needs and the features that will make it most practical for your purposes. A good general-purpose multimeter will handle troubleshooting of most low-voltage systems. The basic multimeter should enable you to measure—within a good range—DC and AC voltages, DC current, and resistance. Some digital meters also include AC current measurement functions. All meters are equipped with two test leads, usually one black and one red. The test ends of the leads may have probe tips or, in some cases, an alligator clip on the black lead and a probe tip on the red lead.

USING THE METER

Different meters vary in the functions that are available with them. I will outline the basics of each function in the hope that the simplicity of operating a meter will encourage you to obtain and use one.

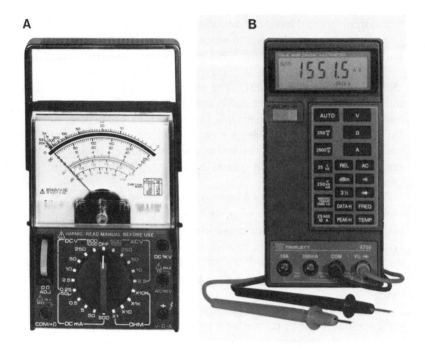

Figure 9–1.   Two types of multimeters. (A) Analogue. (Courtesy of Simpson Electric Co.) (B) Digital. (Courtesy of Triplett Corp.)

Voltage Measurements

The purpose of the *voltmeter* function is to measure voltage across two points of a circuit. Voltage can be defined as the difference in electrical pressure between two points. It is also called potential difference and electromotive force (EMF).

Usually, the selector switch on a meter provides both AC and DC measurement functions, with a range selection available for each function. There is also a positive and a negative input terminal on the meter, normally identified by one of the methods shown in Figure 9–2.

The test leads are color-coded, one red and one black. The normal convention is to connect the red lead to the positive terminal and the black lead to the negative terminal.

When measuring DC voltage, polarity must be observed. The polar-

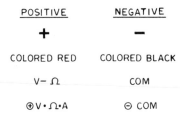

Figure 9–2.   Standard multimeter terminal identifications. (*Note:* Some meters have a separate input terminal for current measurement.)

ity of the circuit might be identified by the marking on a component (+ or −) or by color-coded wiring. Color coding may vary, but it is conventional to have common or negative (−) wired in black and positive (+) wired in red. If the polarity of a DC circuit cannot be identified, one test lead probe can be held on a test point and the other probe quickly tapped on the other test point. It is good practice to apply the common (black) lead first. On analogue meters, the pointer will move below the "O" mark, indicating that you have polarity reversed and that you must swap the positions of your probes to be correctly polarized. Digital meters will read the voltage either way, indicating on the display the polarity you are reading. When using the AC voltage function, polarity need not be observed. Either probe may be connected to either test point.

If the voltage value being measured is not known, it is advisable to set the selector to the highest range on the function (AC or DC) selected. You may then switch down until a satisfactory reading is observed.

If high voltage is applied when the selector is on a low-voltage range, damage may occur to the meter. Voltage readings are always taken with the circuit power turned on. Use extreme caution when measuring voltages of 120 and above. Figures 9–3 and 9–4 show simple voltage measurements being taken. The dark dots in the schematics indicate possible solder joints within the circuits. Readings must be taken with the test probes touching uninsulated junctions or bare wire. If no uninsulated place can be found to place the probes, the following procedure is commonly used: Shut the power off to the circuit. Drive a sewing needle through the insulation into the metal

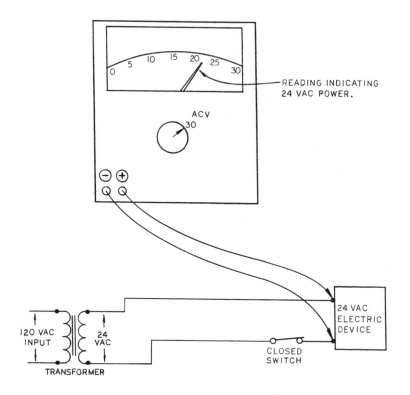

Figure 9–3. Voltage reading being taken on an AC circuit.

wire of one lead. Repeat the process for the second lead. Be careful that the needles do not touch each other or any grounded object. Turn the power back on and take the measurement by placing the probes on the needles. Shut the power off and remove the needles. No damage should be done to the insulation because of the small diameter of the needles. If in doubt, tape the area where the needle entered the insulation.

Current Measurements

The *ammeter* function is used to measure the current being used by a load, or loads, in a circuit. Current can be defined as the result of a

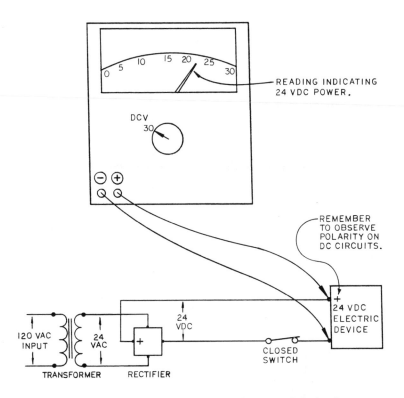

Figure 9—4.   Voltage reading being taken on a DC circuit.

movement of electric charges. The unit of measurement for current is the ampere (amp).

Although most multimeters will measure DC current, many will not measure AC current. Do not attempt to measure AC current unless your meter has that specific function. Most digital meters have both DC and AC current functions.

The test leads should be placed in the correct terminals and the selector set to the desired function—DCA for DC current measurement or ACA for AC current measurement.

When measuring DC current with analogue meters, polarity must be observed. If circuit polarity is not known, it is best to determine polarity on the voltmeter function as previously described. This will prevent possible damage to the meter. In AC circuits, polarity need not be observed.

It is recommended that you start at a high range setting and switch down until a satisfactory reading is observed. When measuring current, the meter must be in series with the load. See Figures 9–5 and 9–6 for examples of this arrangement for current measurements.

Cut power to the system and open up the circuit at a convenient place. Connect the test probes in their proper positions and apply

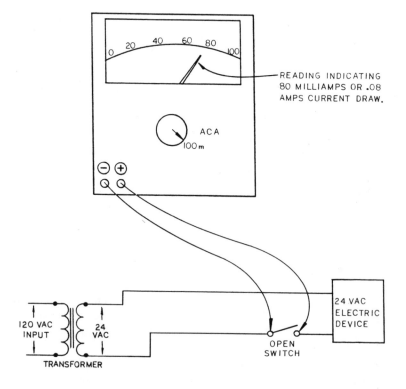

Figure 9–5. Current reading being taken on an AC circuit. (Note that with the switch open, the meter itself is completing the circuit.)

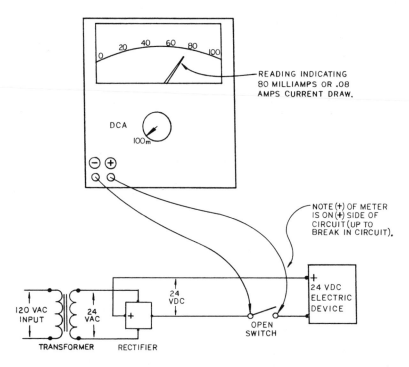

Figure 9–6. Current reading being taken on a DC circuit. (Note that with the switch open, the meter itself is completing the circuit.)

power to the circuit. You should now be measuring the current draw at that particular place in the circuit.

Resistance Measurements

The *ohmmeter* function is used to measure the resistance in a circuit. Resistance is defined as the opposition to the flow of current in a circuit. The measurement unit of resistance is the ohm, often indicated by the Greek letter omega (Ω). You can measure the resistance that a single component offers to the current flow or the resistance of an entire circuit.

Unlike voltage and current measurements, the power to the circuit must be shut off when measuring resistance. It is advisable to discharge all capacitors in a circuit, to remove all batteries, and to unplug all line cords.

The ohmmeter function requires its own power source to provide low current to pass through the subject under test. This current is supplied by a battery located inside the meter. When they are not in use, meters without an on/off switch should not be left in the ohmmeter function, as it will drain the battery power. A "zero" adjustment is provided to compensate for the power lost in the battery over a period of time.

Analogue meters vary as to whether the ohmmeter scale will read left to right or right to left. Consult your operator's manual for the correct procedure to "zero" your meter before starting a measurement.

With the test leads in their proper terminals, place the selector to one of the ohm range positions. It is best to select a range that allows you to read the resistance near the middle of the scale. Check to ensure that all power is off in the circuit. The test probes are placed across the circuit or component under test, as shown in Figure 9–7. Polarity need not be observed in resistance measurements.

When a component has very little resistance, you will get a low reading; conversely, high resistance will give you high reading. You may have to run through all the ranges until you find a range that gives you a mid-scale reading. Remember to "zero" the meter for the range you select to obtain an accurate reading.

If the pointer does not move in any range, you are measuring across an "open" circuit, indicating a disconnection or break in the circuit or component. (This may be a "o" or "infinite" reading on your analogue scale, depending on the type of meter being used.)

If the pointer deflects across the entire scale, you are measuring across a "short" circuit, indicating that the component may be shorted to ground or that the circuit is improperly wired. (This again may be a "o" or "infinite" reading on your scale.)

In certain cases, it may be necessary to disconnect one side of a component being tested in a circuit to prevent interference in the reading from other parts of the circuit.

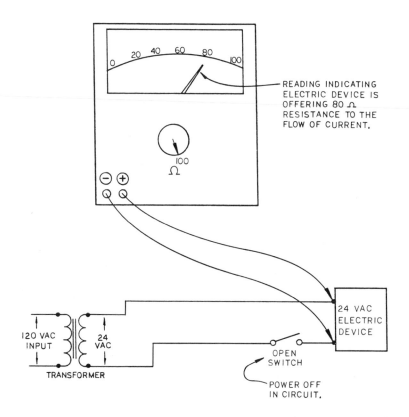

Figure 9–7.   Resistance reading being taken on a component in a circuit.

REVIEW

Use of a multimeter can save you time and money. A multimeter functions as (1) a voltmeter, to measure voltage (the difference in electrical pressure between two points); (2) an ammeter, to measure current (movement or flow of electrical charges); and (3) an ohmmeter, to measure resistance (opposition to, or control of, current flow). Select a meter that best suits your needs.

Use caution when working with or near high voltages. Observe polarity when measuring DC voltage and current. Do not attempt to measure AC current unless your meter is capable of doing so. When measuring resistance, make sure that circuit power is off.

Appendix A

Codes and Standards

No attempt has been made in this text to explain, argue, or philosophize on the multitude of codes and standards used throughout the country. Rather, I will only list and briefly define some of the most widely used codes and standards that affect the electric locking industry.

The main objective of these codes and standards is to provide for public safety through guidelines established for the manufacture and use of various types of equipment. Manufacturers, builders, and installers all have codes and standards to follow in their particular areas of interest. Codes and standards also provide a format for quality and standardization throughout the industry.

In your personal experience, you will be faced with codes and standards not listed herein, and you may never have to deal with some of those that are listed. Code use tends to be regional, and every state, county, and city must be dealt with individually for local approvals and restrictions. However, most codes are based on national code publications.

When pursuing a particular project, you must first determine the codes you will confront and interpret their requirements properly. At times, you may find it necessary to deviate from the scope of local codes. You may even find a lack of any reference for the use of some new product or technology.

Although development of new methods in the security field is encouraged, it is often difficult to stimulate acceptance of code changes or of additions and deletions based on new developments. You must be prepared to become the "salesperson" for a proposed change or departure from an existing code. The authority having jurisdiction—that is, the building inspector, the fire marshal, or whoever will make the final approval of the installation—is the person you will have to convince.

You must prepare your case thoroughly, with public safety foremost in your presentation. In some instances, the change you seek may be in an area of interest to others. Your knowledge of the latest developments in the security field may gain you local, regional, or even national support from interested organizations and manufacturers. Occasionally, in an effort to gain wider acceptance of a common conception, these parties may provide help in presenting and interpreting a new or existing code not adopted by local authorities.

You may find that some of the associations in the following lists have been used as a reference for or form the basis of codes in your area. It is advisable that you familiarize yourself with the actual code or standard used in order to recognize any variations that local authorities may have adopted. In some cases, the local code may be based on outdated material, or later technology may be available to help you influence the authority having jurisdiction to accept a deviation.

BUILDING CODES

The organizations listed here publish codes referred to as the model building codes. They represent the three major building codes that influence the standards for most of this country.

Each organization publishes codes that are available for adoption into local codes. Although local governments may write their own codes, the tendency is to take advantage of the technical expertise offered by these code groups. The codes may form a local code in whole, may be modified to suit local requirements, or may appear only as a reference.

The three code groups tend to be regionalized, but they are not limited to any one part of the country. All share a common goal: the establishment of minimum building and safety standards for the construction of all types of buildings. The differences in the three codes exist partially because they were developed by separate groups of people. Differences also exist because of specific conditions not shared by all regions, such as weather and natural disasters.

The Council of American Building Officials (CABO), through its Board for Coordination of Model Codes, is involved in reviewing differences in these codes. This board's suggestions have prompted uniformity within the codes and with NFPA 101—Life Safety Code. CABO is located at 5205 Leesburg Pike, Falls Church, VA 22041.

BOCA—Basic Building Code
Building Officials and Code Administrators International
4051 W. Flossmoor Road
Country Club Hills, IL 60477
(312)799-2300

Founded in 1915, BOCA membership is mostly made up of building officials, architects, engineers, and industry personnel. It primarily covers the northeastern section of the country and publishes the Basic Building Code every three years, with annual updates.

BOCA is a service organization, providing its members with technical and educational information directed toward the development of safe and efficient building codes.

ICBO—Uniform Building Code
International Conference of Building Officials
5360 Workman Mill Road
Whittier, CA 90601
(213)699-0541

Founded in 1927, ICBO membership includes local government agencies, building professionals, and trade associations. It covers roughly the western half of the country and publishes the Uniform Building Code every three years, with annual updates.

The ICBO provides educational information, training programs, and product evaluation in an effort to promote a uniform code system.

SBCCI—Standard Building Code
Southern Building Code Congress International
900 Montclair Road
Birmingham, AL 35213
(205)591-1953

Founded in 1940, SBCCI members are mostly building officials, with an associate membership of industry personnel and fire officials. It covers roughly the southeastern section of the country, as far west as Texas and Oklahoma, and publishes the Standard Building Code every three years, with annual updates.

The SBCCI provides technical and educational material directed toward establishing minimum requirements for life safety and property protection.

FIRE AND LIFE SAFETY CODES

National Fire Protection Association (NFPA)
Batterymarch Park
Quincy, MA 02269
(617)770-3000

The NFPA was organized in 1896 to promote the science and improve the methods of fire protection and prevention. Its primary concerns are to obtain and circulate information on these subjects and to secure the cooperation of its members in establishing proper safeguards against loss of life and property by fire.

The association is an international charitable, technical, and educational organization. It urges reference to its publications by public authorities in laws, ordinances, regulations or related areas. Adopting authorities should contact the NFPA concerning its licensing provisions whenever they are considering adopting any of its documents, either by reference or by altering the document by deletions, additions, or changes.

The NFPA does not approve, inspect, or certify any installations, procedures, equipment, or materials, nor does it approve or evaluate testing laboratories.

The following codes published by the NFPA affect our industry:

NFC—National Fire Codes

An annual compilation of the codes, standards, recommended practices, manuals, guides, and model laws prepared by technical committees organized under NFPA sponsorship. Volumes 1 through 12 contain documents that have been judged suitable for legal adoption and enforcement. Volumes 13 through 16 contain recommended practices, manuals, and guides that are generally referred to as Good Engineering Practices.

NFPA 101—Life Safety Code

This code originated in the work of the Committee on Safety to Life of the NFPA, appointed in 1913. The committee's work led to the preparation of standards for the construction of stairways, fire escapes, and the like; for fire drills in various occupancies; and for the construction and arrangement of exit facilities for factories, schools, and so on. These standards form the basis of the present code, which addresses itself specifically to requirements influencing safety to life in both new and existing structures. The code is a comprehensive guide to exits and related features of life safety from fire in all classes of occupancy; new material is added as new editions are published. The code is used primarily as a supplement to building codes and has been revised on a three-year schedule since 1967.

NFPA 70—National Electrical Code

Proposed in 1881, the first nationally recommended electrical code was published in 1895. The NFPA assumed sponsorship and control of the National Electrical Code in 1911. The code has been officially endorsed by the American National Standards Institute (ANSI) since 1920. The NFPA has been publishing and distributing the code since 1951. It is the most widely adopted code in the world and is a nationally accepted guide to the safe installation of electrical conductors and equipment. It is the basis for all electrical codes used in this country.

NFPA 80—Fire Doors and Windows

From 1911 through 1941, a standard for the protection of openings in walls and partitions existed under various titles. In 1959, a complete revision was adopted, including a change to its present title. This code provides a standard for the installation of all types of fire doors and windows and for the use of specific hardware on these openings.

HANDICAP CODES

Wider acceptance and stricter enforcement of "handicap codes" require that more attention be focused on this area. Research in barrier-free design resulted in the first design specification to be approved by the American National Standards Institute, ANSI A117.1-1961. The latest standard, ANSI A117.1-1986, is entitled "American National Standard for Buildings and Facilities—providing accessibility and usability for physically handicapped people." The purpose of this standard is to make buildings and facilities accessible to and usable by people with certain physical disabilities. A lack of nationwide uniformity makes it essential that you know the provisions of local codes regarding this area. It is likely that ANSI A117.1 will be the most widely accepted standard as the basis for local handicap codes.

STANDARDS

American National Standards Institute (ANSI)
1430 Broadway
New York, NY 10018
(212)354-3300

In its efforts to create voluntary standards, eliminate duplication, and resolve conflicting standards, ANSI has approved about 4,000 nationally accepted standards. The standards represent a general agreement among manufacturers, distributors, and consumers regarding the best practices over a wide area of the building industry. Through its membership in worldwide organizations, ANSI influences standardization on an international level.

National Electrical Manufacturers' Association (NEMA)
155 East 44th Street
New York City, NY 10017

About the only time you will see reference to NEMA standards will be in conjunction with electrical enclosures. Some of the NEMA grades for this type of equipment are listed in Appendix E.

TESTING LABORATORIES

The function of testing laboratories is to test products submitted by manufacturers and document the results. The tests are done to determine whether the product presents any safety hazard to the public and whether it performs as specified for its intended use. Simulated conditions duplicating actual use situations are often used to test products.

Upon successful completion of testing, a laboratory will certify approval by some method of recognition or listing. It will normally require that the product be "labeled" in a specific manner for as long as the approval is in effect.

Many labs require additional obligations from the manufacturer to keep the certification valid. This is commonly referred to as "follow-up service"; it can include some or all of the following:

In-house inspection: A laboratory inspector will visit a manufacturers' plant periodically to ensure that the product is being built to specifications as approved.

Product sampling: The laboratory may purchase the product on the open market and inspect it for compliance to the approval.

Field inspection: Laboratory inspectors may visit an actual installation to ensure that the product is used in compliance with approved methods and procedures.

Testing labs vary somewhat in their areas of investigation, and local codes may insist on product approval by a specific laboratory. Like codes, testing tends to be specified on a regional basis.

Underwriters Laboratories, Inc. (UL)
333 Pfingsten Road
Northbrook, IL 60062
(312)272-8800

Founded in 1894 and chartered as a nonprofit organization, UL is one of the most widely recognized and accepted testing labs in this country. Its laboratories examine and test devices, systems, and materials to determine their relation to hazards to public safety.

Factory Mutual Research Corp. (FM)
1151 Boston-Providence Turnpike
Norwood, MA 02062
(617)762-4300

A national testing lab for over a century, FM is involved in determining whether equipment, materials, and services meet certain requirements. Submitted items must perform satisfactorily, reliably, and repeatedly as intended. Production of such items must be under high-quality control conditions.

Warnock Hersey International, Inc. (WHI)
770 Ritchie Highway, Suite W-25
Severna Park, MD 21146
(301)647-0773

Established in 1888 in Canada, WHI is an independent certification and testing agency that provides fire testing and technical services to industry and government. Its Fire Laboratories Division has been recognized throughout North America for more than a decade. Among other services, it provides fire testing, certification, and labeling for doors and frames and related hardware. WHI maintains regional offices throughout the United States and Canada.

CANADIAN CODES AND STANDARDS

The following organizations in Canada closely parallel those of this country. Although they are totally independent of organizations in the United States, they offer many of the same services.

Building Codes

National Research Council
Montreal Road
Ottawa, ON K1A OR6
(613)993-9101

The National Building Code and the National Fire Code are published through the Associate Committee on the National Building Code (ACNBC) and the Associate Committee on the National Fire Code

(ACNFC). These advisory codes may be adopted by municipal or provincial authorities.

Testing Laboratories

Underwriters Laboratories of Canada (ULC)
7 Crouse Road
Scarborough, ON M1R 3A9
(416)757-3611

Incorporated in 1920 as a nonprofit testing lab, ULC examines, tests, and classifies devices, materials, and systems. It also develops and publishes standards for fire, accident, or property hazards. ULC is not affiliated with Underwriters Laboratories, Inc.

Canadian Standards Association (CSA)
178 Rexdale Boulevard
Rexdale, ON M9W 1R3
(416)744-4129

Incorporated in 1919 as a nonprofit organization, CSA provides examination, testing, and inspection of submitted products or systems. Certification is granted upon compliance with applicable standards for safety and performance.

Warnock Hersey Professional Services, Ltd.
3210 American Drive
Mississauga, ON L47 1B3
(416)678-7820

Warnock Hersey has provided independent testing services since 1888. It provides commercial fire rating, testing, and labeling services for manufacturers of doors, wall systems, and building components. Recognized throughout North America, it maintains regional offices in the United States and Canada.

Appendix B

Door Handing and Frequency of Use

DOOR HANDING

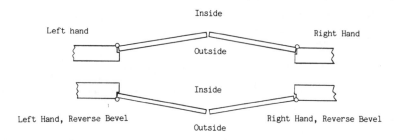

DOOR HANDS DETERMINED FROM OUTSIDE

Figure B–1. U.S. standardization procedure for door handing.

FREQUENCY OF USE

Table B–1.   Frequency of Door Use

Type of Building and Door	Expected Frequency[a]	
	Daily	Yearly
Large department store entrance	5,000	1,500,000
Large office building entrance	4,000	1,200,000
Theater entrance	1,000	450,000
Schoolhouse entrance	1,250	225,000
Schoolhouse toilet door	1,250	225,000
Store or bank entrance	500	150,000
Office building toilet door	400	118,000
Schoolhouse corridor door	80	15,000
Office building corridor door	75	22,000
Store toilet door	60	18,000
Dwelling entrance	40	15,000
Dwelling toilet door	25	9,000
Dwelling corridor door	10	3,600
Dwelling closet door	6	2,200

[a] Number of operations (opening and closing = 1 cycle) of one leaf or door.

Appendix C

Common Abbreviations

The following abbreviations are a mixture of electrical and hardware terms that often appear on documents regarding electronic security.

A	amperes
AA	alternate action
AC	alternating current
AH	ampere/hours
AHF	adjustable holding force
AL	aluminum
AMP	amperes
AN	anodized
ATD	adjustable time delay
AWG	American Wire Gauge
BP	bolt position
BPS	bolt position switch
BR	brass
CONT	continuous duty
CR	control relay
CT	center tap
CYL	cylinder

D	diode
DA	delayed action
dB	decibel
DC	direct current
DPDT	double pole, double throw
DPST	double pole, single throw
DR	door
DSS	door status switch
ER	emergency release
F	flush
FEH	fire exit hardware
FR	frame
HM	hollow metal
Hz	Hertz (cycles per second)
INT	intermittent duty
J	junction box
KA	keyed alike
KO	knock out
LC	line cord
LH	left hand
LHR	left hand reverse bevel
M	magnet
MAINT	maintained contact
MOM	momentary contact
MR	manual release
MS	machine screw
MSC	manual station control
NC	normally closed
NO	normally open
NS	narrow stile
PB	pushbutton
PS	power supply
R	resistor
RB	rectifier bridge
RFI	radio frequency interference
RH	right hand
RHR	right hand reverse bevel
SO	silent operation
SPDT	single pole, double throw

SPNC	single pole, normally closed
SPNO	single pole, normally open
SPST	single pole, single throw
SS	stainless steel
STL	steel
SW	switch
UPS	uninterruptible power system
V	volt
VA	volt/ampere
W	watt
WP	weatherproof
WD	wood door
WS	wood screw

Appendix D

Electronic Symbols

You will often be confronted with drawings called schematics, wiring diagrams, or some similar term, that will specify electronic components by symbols. Some standard electronic symbols are shown in Figure D–1.

NAME	SYMBOL	REFERENCE SIGN
Alarm (horn, siren, etc.)		None
Battery	6V / BT1	BT
Capacitor	(NON POLAR) C1 (POLARIZED) + C2	C
Circuit breaker	2 A / CB1	CB

Figure D–1.   Schematic symbols.

NAME	SYMBOL	REFERENCE SIGN
Connector (120 VAC)	OUTLET PLUG	None
Connector (general)	P1 S1 A (PIN#)	P,S
Diode (general)	D1	D
Diode, light emitting (LED)	D2	D
Diode, zener	D3	D
Fuse	F1 2A	F
Ground	(EARTH) (CHASSIS) (COM.BUS)	GND
Light or lamp	L1 R (COLOR)	L

Figure D–1. (*continued*)

NAME	SYMBOL	REFERENCE SIGN
Load (general)		None
Potentiometer (resistor with adjustable tap)	P1	P
Rectifier (full wave bridge)	RB1 AC OR RB2	RB
Relay coil	②(1CR)⑦ (RELAY PIN #)	CR
Relay contacts	C① 1CR-1 ③NO ④NC	CR
Resistor	R1 (FIXED) R2 (VARIABLE)	R
Switch (general)	(NO) (NC) (SPDT) (DPDT)	SW (general) PB (pushbutton) T (toggle)

Figure D–1.   (*continued*)

NAME	SYMBOL	REFERENCE SIGN
Terminal block	TB1 ① ② ③ ④ ⑤	TB
Test point	TP1	TP
Transformer	T1	T
Transistor	Q1	Q
Wires, shielded		None
Wires, twisted	TWIST (PAIR)	None
Wiring	(CONNECTED) (NOT CONNECTED) OR	None

Figure D–1.   (*continued*)

Appendix E

Electrical Enclosures

You will often hear reference made to NEMA grades for electrical enclosures used in different environments. The following are some of the types of enclosures available for use with electrical equipment. The list is not intended to be a complete representation of National Electrical Manufacturers Association (NEMA) Standards for Enclosures.

NEMA Type 1—General-Purpose.   Indoor enclosures are intended primarily to prevent accidental contact of personnel with the enclosed equipment in indoor applications wherever oil, dust, or water is not a problem.

NEMA Type 2—Dripproof.   Indoor enclosures are intended for use indoors to protect the enclosed equipment against falling noncorrosive liquids and falling dirt.

NEMA Type 3—Dusttight, Raintight, and Sleet- and Ice-Resistant.   Outdoor enclosures are intended for use outdoors to protect the enclosed equipment against windblown dust and water.

NEMA Type 3R—Rainproof and Sleet- and Ice-Resistant.   Outdoor enclosures are intended for use outdoors to protect the enclosed equipment against rain and are constructed so that the accumulation and melting of sleet (ice) will not damage the enclosure and its external mechanisms.

NEMA Type 3S—Dusttight, Raintight, and Sleet- and Ice-Proof.   Outdoor enclosures are intended for use outdoors to protect the enclosed equipment against windblown dust and water and to provide for its operation when the enclosure is covered by external ice or sleet.

NEMA Type 4—Watertight and Dusttight.   Indoor and outdoor enclosures are intended for use indoors or outdoors to protect the enclosed equipment against splashing water, seepage of water, falling of hose-directed water, and severe external condensation.

NEMA Type 4X—Watertight, Dusttight, and Corrosion-Resistant.   Indoor or outdoor enclosures have the same provisions as Type 4 enclosures and, in addition, are corrosion-resistant.

NEMA Type 9—Class II, Group E, F, or G—Indoor Hazardous Locations.   Air-break equipment enclosures are intended for use indoors, in atmospheres defined as Class II and Group E, F, or G in the National Electrical Code, to prevent the entrance of explosive amounts of hazardous dust.

NEMA Type 12—Industrial Use—Dusttight and Driptight.   Indoor enclosures are intended for use indoors to protect the enclosed equipment against fibers, flyings, lint, dust and dirt, and light splashing, seepage, dripping, and external condensation of noncorrosive liquids.

NEMA Type 13—Oiltight and Dusttight.   Indoor enclosures are intended for use indoors primarily to house pilot devices such as limit switches, foot switches, pushbuttons, selector switches, pilot lights, and so on, and to protect these devices against lint and dust, seepage, external condensation, and spraying of water, oil, or coolant.

Appendix F

Ohm's Law

Ohm's Law establishes the relationships between voltage, current, and resistance. It allows you to determine one of these components if you know or can measure the other two. It is expressed in the formula $I = E/R$, where I equals current (amps), E equals voltage (volts), and R equals resistance (ohms). Figure F–1 will help prompt your memory when using the formula.

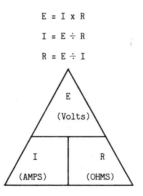

$$E = I \times R$$
$$I = E \div R$$
$$R = E \div I$$

Figure F–1.   Ohm's Law. Cover the block for the component you are seeking, and perform the calculations.

Appendix G

Directories

PRODUCTS

The following lists are based primarily on electric lock manufacturers' product lines. Any omissions are due to lack of available information. Electric hinges and transformers have been included for your convenience. Access controls and monitoring devices are available from many sources, so the list here is not intended to be complete.

Access Controls

Alarm Lock
Architectural Control Systems
Continental Instruments
Corbin
Edwards
Folger Adam
Locknetics
Magnegard
Reliable Security Systems

Rixson
Rofu
Securitron Magnalock
Security Door Control
Security Engineering
Trine
Von Duprin
Yale

Hinges—Electric

Folger Adam
Hager
Lawrence Brothers

McKinney
Rixson
Stanley

Locks—Bolts

Alarm Lock
Folger Adam
Locknetics
Rofu

Security Door Control
Security Engineering
Yale

Locks—Electromagnetic

Locknetics
Magnegard
Reliable Security Systems
Rixson
Rofu

Securitron Magnalock
Security Door Control
Security Engineering
Von Duprin

Locks—Electromechanical

Alarm Lock
Architectural Control Systems
R. R. Brink
Corbin
Folger Adam
Sargent

Sargent & Greenleaf
Schlage
Security Door Control
Von Duprin
Yale

Locks—Strikes

Adams Rite
Continental Instruments
Corbin
Edwards
Folger Adam
Hanchett Entry Systems

Precision Hardware
Rofu
Sargent & Greenleaf
Security Door Control
Trine
Von Duprin

Monitoring Devices

Alarm Lock
Architectural Control Systems
Continental Instruments
Corbin
Edwards
Folger Adam
Locknetics
Magnegard
Reliable Security Systems

Rixson
Rofu
Securitron Magnalock
Security Door Control
Security Engineering
Trine
Von Duprin
Yale

Panic Devices—Electric

Adams Rite
Door Controls International
Von Duprin

Pivots—Electric

Rixson

Power Supplies

Architectural Control Systems
Ault
Locknetics
Reliable Security Systems

Rixson
Securitron Magnalock
Security Engineering
Von Duprin

Power Transfers

Alarm Lock
Locknetics
Rixson

Rofu
Trine
Von Duprin

Transformers

Adams Rite
Alarm Lock
Ault
Basler
Corbin

Edwards
Hanchett Entry Systems
Locknetics
Magnegard
Reliable Security Systems

Security Door Control   Stancor
Security Engineering   Von Duprin

MANUFACTURERS

The following is primarily a listing of electric lock manufacturers. Any omissions are due to the lack of available information. Several electric hinge and transformer manufacturers have been included for your convenience.

Adams Rite Mfg. Co.
P.O. Box 1301
4040 S. Capitol Avenue
City of Industry, CA 91749
(213)699-0511

Alarm Lock Corp.
Division of Emergency Product
  Corp.
P.O. Box 2001
10 Old Bloomfield Avenue
Pine Brook, NJ 07058
(201)882-8010

Architectural Control Systems,
  Inc.
8148 Brentwood Ind. Drive
St. Louis, MO 63144
(314)781-0301

Ault Inc.
1600 Freeway Blvd.
Minneapolis, MN 55430
(612)560-9300

Basler Electric
Box 269
Highland, IL 62249
(618)654-2341

R. R. Brink Locking Systems, Inc.
500 Earl Road
Shorewood, IL 60436
(815)744-7000

Continental Instruments Corp.
70 Hopper Street
Westbury, NY 11590
(516)334-0900

Corbin Electronic Hardware
Division of Emhart Ind., Inc.
225 Episcopal Road
Berlin, CT 06037
(203)225-7411

Door Controls International
727 W. Ellsworth Road, Bldg. 7
Ann Arbor, MI 48104
(313)665-8818
1-800-742-3634

Edwards
A Unit of General Signal
Box F
195 Farmington Avenue
Farmington, CT 06032
(203)678-0410

Folger Adam Company
16300 W. 103rd Street
Lemont, IL 60439
(312)739-3900

Hager Hinge Company
139 Victor Street
St. Louis, MO 63104
(314)772-4400

Hanchett Entry Systems, Inc.
P.O. Box 7636
Phoenix, AZ 85011
4112 N. 20th Street
Phoenix, AZ 85016
(602)264-6386

Lawrence Brothers, Inc.
2 First Avenue
P.O. Box 538
Sterling, IL 61081

Locknetics Security Products
A Division of H. B. Ives
131 Leeder Hill Dr., Bldg. 261
Hamden, CT 06517
(203)248-3833

Magnegard Division
33 South Service Road
Jericho, NY 11753
(516)333-6111

McKinney
Subsidiary of Kidde, Inc.
820 Davis Street
Scranton, PA 18505
(717)346-7551

Precision Hardware, Inc.
P.O. Box 09245
10053 W. Fort Street
Detroit, MI 48209
(313)843-1850

Reliable Security Systems, Inc.
10604 Beaver Dam Road
Cockeysville, MD 21030
(301)666-3316

Rixson-Firemark, Inc.
A Division of Conrac Corp.
9100 W. Belmont Avenue
Franklin Park, IL 60131
(312)671-5670

Rofu International Corp.
3725 Old Conejo Road
Newbury Park, CA 91320
(805)499-0316

Sargent & Company
Division of Kidde, Inc.
100 Sargent Drive
New Haven, CT 06511
(203)562-2151

Sargent & Greenleaf, Inc.
1 Security Drive
Nicholasville, KY 40356
(606)885-9411

Schlage Lock Company
P.O. Box 3324
San Francisco, CA 94119
(415)467-1100

Securitron Magnalock Corp.
1815 W. 205th Street, Suite 105
Torrance, CA 90501
(213)618-0204

Security Door Controls
P.O. Box 6219
Westlake Village, CA 91359
(818)996-6584

Security Engineering, Inc.
P.O. Box 9337
560 Birch Street
Forestville, CT 06010
(203)584-9158

Stancor Products
131 Godfrey Street
Logansport, IN 46947
(219)722-2244

Stanley
195 Lake Street
New Britain, CT 06050
(203)225-5111

Trine Products Corp.
Square D Company
1430 Ferris Place
Bronx, NY 10461
(212)829-4796

Von Duprin, Inc.
2720 Tobey Drive
Indianapolis, IN 46219
(317)637-5521

Yale Security Division
Scovill
P.O. Box 25288
Charlotte, NC 28212
(704)283-2101

Glossary

access control   The means of influencing and regulating the flow of persons through a door (entry and/or exit).

actuator   The mechanism of the switch or switch enclosure that operates the contacts.

adjustable   The ability to change or alter the time delay or other parameter by means of an adjustment, such as a potentiometer, a resistor, or a switch.

alarm   A device used to indicate an emergency or other specific condition.

alligator clip   A mechanical device, shaped like the jaws of an alligator, used as a temporary connection on the end of a test lead or jumper wire.

alternating current (AC)   An electric current that reverses its direction regularly and continually. The voltage alternates its polarity and direction of current flow negative to positive. AC current increases to a peak, decreases through zero, and peaks in the opposite direction. AC current flows back and forth in the conductor and is expressed in cycles per second, or Hertz (Hz).

ambient temperature   The temperature of the air immediately surrounding a device or object.

American National Standards Institute (ANSI)   A federation of trade, technical, and professional organizations, government agencies, and consumer groups that coordinates standards development, publishes standards, and operates a voluntary certification program.

American Society for Testing Materials (ASTM) An organization that tests materials and attempts to set standards on various materials for industry.

American Wire Gauge (AWG) The standard system in the United States for designating wire size (diameter of metal).

ampere (amp) The unit of measurement for the rate of electrical current flow, characterized by the symbols I (in Ohm's law formulas) or A. One ampere is the current flowing through one ohm of resistance at one volt potential.

ampere/hour (AH) A measurement of a battery's capacity. One ampere of current flowing for one hour equals one ampere/hour.

annunciator An audible and/or visual signaling device.

arc An electrical current through air or across the surface of an insulator associated with high voltage. An arc usually occurs when a contact is opened, deenergizing an inductive load. Arcing of a contact will limit its life.

armor A metal jacket surrounding wires for mechanical protection.

authorized release device A device that, when activated, allows authorized persons to enter or exit monitored and controlled openings without triggering an alarm. The authorized passage release may be a keyed switch, a card reader, a digital code reader, and so forth.

battery standby A means of automatically switching over to stored battery power during local primary power failure.

bell wire 18 gauge insulated solid copper wire, used for making doorbell and thermostat connections in homes.

block diagram A drawing that shows the relationship of equipment in a system. Blocks used to represent each piece of equipment are arranged into a system diagram that shows their physical or operational relation to each other.

bolt The projectable member of a lock or latch mechanism that engages the door frame and the strike. (See *deadbolt* and *latchbolt*.)

bolt position switch A miniature switch used on or in a locking device to monitor whether the locking bolt is in the locked (projected) or unlocked (retracted) position.

box strike A strike in which the latchbolt recess is enclosed or boxed, thus covering the opening in the jamb.

break   To open an electrical circuit.

breakdown voltage   The voltage at which the insulation between two conductors is destroyed.

brownout   Low line voltage, which can cause misoperation of and possible damage to equipment. For example, a motor that tries to start at low voltage can actually be in a lock-rotor condition and can overheat.

bus   A common return path in electric circuits.

cable   A group of insulated conductors in a common jacket.

cable clamp   A device used to give mechanical support to a wire bundle or cable.

cable tie   A beltlike plastic strip that loops around bundles of cables or insulated wires to hold them together.

cam   A rotating eccentric piece attached to the end of a cylinder plug to actuate a lock or latch mechanism.

case   A housing for a lock mechanism.

chip   A microminiature electronic circuit on a tiny silicon wafer or other conductive material.

circuit   The path through which electrical energy flows.

circuit, closed   (1) An electrical circuit in which current normally flows until interrupted by the opening of a switch or a switch-type electronic component. (2) A circuit or switch in which the contacts are closed during normal operation.

circuit, open   (1) An electrical circuit in which current does not flow until permitted by the closing of a switch or a switch-type electronic component. (2) A circuit or switch in which the contacts are open during normal operation.

closure   The point at which two contacts meet to complete a circuit.

coaxial cable   A cable consisting of two cylindrical conductors with a common axis. The two conductors are separated by a dielectric. The outer conductor, normally at ground potential, acts as a return path for current flowing through the center conductor and prevents energy radiation from the cable. The outer conductor, or shield, is also commonly used to prevent external radiation from affecting the current flowing in the inner conductor. The outer shield or conductor consists of woven strands of wire or is a metal sheath.

code bypass   A means of opening a door from inside the protected area (usually by pressing a button) without entering a key or code in the key reader.

coded card   A plastic card (usually polyvinyl chloride) that has a combination (three to six digits) secreted in its design either in a series of small magnets or on magnetic tape (mag stripe).

coil, electric   Successive turns of insulated wire that create a magnetic field when an electric current is passed through them.

cold solder joint   A solder connection that exhibits poor wetting and a grayish, porous appearance due to insufficient heat, inadequate cleaning prior to soldering, or excessive impurities in the solder solution.

conductance   The ability of an electrical conductor to pass current; the reciprocal of resistance.

conductivity   The capability of a material to carry electrical current—usually expressed as a percentage of copper conductivity (copper being 100 percent).

conductor   Material with the ability to carry electric current. The term is also used for an electric wire.

conduit   A tube or trough for protecting electrical wires or cables. It may be a solid or flexible tube in which insulated electrical wires are run.

connector   Generally, any device used to provide rapid connect/disconnect service for electrical cable and wire terminations.

contact chatter (contact bounce)   A condition that sometimes occurs on closure of two contacts. When a mechanical contact closes, the contacts make and break several times before a stable closed condition is established. Bounce or chatter can also be caused by external vibration or shock on a closed contact.

contacts   Electrically conductive points, or sets of points, used to make or break an electrical circuit mechanically.

continuity   The state of being complete and uninterrupted, like a normally closed circuit.

continuity check   A test performed on a length of wire or cable to determine whether the electrical current flows continuously throughout the length.

continuous duty   Refers to a device or a control that can operate continuously with no off or rest periods.

continuous duty locking unit   An electric lock equipped with a heavy-duty solenoid that can be energized indefinitely.

control box   A sheetmetal enclosure that contains electronic and electromechanical controls and circuitry.

crimp   To compress (deform) a connector barrel around a cable in order to make an electrical connection.

crimp termination   A connection in which a metal sleeve is secured to a conductor by mechanically crimping the sleeve with pliers, presses, or automated crimping machines. Splices, terminals, and multicontact connectors are typical terminating devices attached by crimping. Crimping is suitable for all wire types.

current   The flow of electrons through an electrical conductor. Current is measured in amperes.

current-carrying capacity   The maximum current an insulated conductor can safely carry without exceeding its insulation and jacket temperature limitations.

cycle (frequency)   The number of times per second the current in an alternating current system reverses its direction of flow. The standard commercial current in the United States is 60-cycle (60Hz).

cylinder   A housing that contains a tumbler mechanism and a keyway plug that can be turned only by the correct key. It includes a cam or spindle to transmit rotary action to a lock or latch mechanism. For security and keying versatility, authorities generally specify a pin-tumbler cylinder of no fewer than five pins. The two types of cylinders—the mortise cylinder (round, threaded housing) and the bored lock cylinder (sometimes called a cylinder insert)—both provide the same functional value of security and convenience and are often included in the same keying system. (See *keying*.)

deadbolt   A bolt operated manually and not actuated by springs. When locked, the bolt cannot be forced back. A deadbolt is operated (projected and retracted) by a key cylinder or lever handle.

deadlatch   A latch in which the latchbolt is positively held in the projected position by an auxiliary mechanism.

decibel (dB)   An increment of measurement used to compare measured levels of sound energy (intensity) to the apparent level detected by the human ear, expressed as a logarithmic ratio. A sound that has 10 times the energy of another sound is said to be 10 decibels louder; 100 times the energy is 20 decibels louder; 1,000 times the energy is 30 decibels louder; and so on. Decibel levels are correctly expressed as the number of decibels at a measured distance from the course of sound (for example, 125 dB at 10 feet).

deenergize   To remove power.

delay   A period of time before or during an event.

delay on break   A term used to describe a mode of operation relative to timing devices. The delay begins when the initiate switch is opened (delay on break of initiate switch).

delay on energization   A term used to describe a mode of operation relative to timing devices. The delay begins when the initiate switch is closed or on application of power to the input.

delay on make   Same as *delay on energization.*

dielectric   Any insulating material between two conductors that permits electrostatic attraction and repulsion to take place across it.

digital printer   A device that receives electronically coded signals and prints this information on a paper tape.

DIP switch   A miniature switch used to program, set, or change circuit functions. DIP is an abbreviation for the dual-in-line package, which houses the switch.

direct current (DC)   Electrical current that travels in only one direction and has negative ($-$) and positive ($+$) polarity. It may or may not have an AC ripple component. DC sources that are unfiltered should be referred to as full-wave or half-wave rectified AC.

door status switch   A DSS is a switch used to monitor whether a door is in an opened or closed position.

double pole, double throw (DPDT)   A term used to describe a switch or relay output contact form (2 form C) in which two separate switches are operating simultaneously, each with a normally open and normally closed contact and a common connection. This form is used to make and break two separate circuits.

dry contact   Metallic points making (shorting) or breaking (opening) a circuit. The switched circuit must have its own source of power and is merely routed through the dry contacts.

duty cycle   The percentage of on time or operating time of a device. For example, a device that is on for one minute and off for nine minutes is operating at a 10 percent duty cycle.

electric door strike   An electric door locking device (usually solenoid-operated) that will unlock the door when electrical power is applied to it. A fail-safe configuration will operate in the reverse condition (i.e., normally locked when power is applied and unlocked when power is interrupted).

electromagnet   A coil of wire, usually wound on an iron core, that produces a strong magnetic field when current is sent through the coil.

electromagnetic   Pertaining to combined electric and magnetic fields associated with movements of electrons through conductors.

electromotive force (EMF)   Pressure or voltage; the force that causes current to flow in a circuit.

emergency release   An optional feature of a lock that provides a means of overriding the lock and retracting the bolt in an emergency. It can be operated either mechanically or electrically.

encapsulant   A material, usually epoxy, used to encase and seal all components in an electronic circuit.

end-of-line (EOL) resistor   Resistance in a supervised circuit, usually at the farthest point from the alarm control unit, restricting the flow of current to a known value, which is monitored. Shorting the circuit in an attempt to bypass protective devices in the loop (e.g., door contacts) will create increased flow of current and cause an alarm. Opening (breaking) the circuit also triggers an alarm if the system is armed or a supervisory signal if the system is disarmed.

energize   To apply power.

explosion-proof device   Any device, such as a contact switch, that is enclosed in an explosion-proof housing to help prevent possible sparking in potentially volatile environments.

external adjustment   A device, outside the control, that is used to alter or change the controlled parameter (e.g., an external potentiometer with a time-delay control).

factory calibration   Tuning or altering of a control circuit by the manufacturer to bring the circuit into specification; normally stated as a percentage deviation.

factory fixed   Refers to adjustment made by the manufacturer and not accessible to the user.

fail-safe lock   An electric lock that automatically unlocks with any power interruption.

fail-secure lock   An electric lock that requires power to unlock.

fast-on terminal   A solderless, easy-to-use, female/male push-on terminal that comes in various sizes. It is a common termination for controls and is widely used in automotive, appliance, and other OEM equipment.

fire door latch A latch that has a ¾-inch throw and an antifriction retractor.

flasher A control in which the output to the load (normally a lamp) is turned on and off repeatedly at a given rate of operation or flashes per minute (FPM).

flux (1) The lines of force that make up an electrostatic field. (2) The rate of flow of energy across or through a surface. (3) A substance used to promote or facilitate fusion, such as a material that removes oxides from surfaces to be joined by soldering or welding.

form C contact A switch mechanism that contains three terminals (normally open, common, and normally closed).

frequency The number of complete operations or cycles that take place within a given period of time (normally one second), as in the AC line frequency of 60Hz (60 cycles per second).

full-wave A term used for both AC and DC voltages, suggesting that both halves of the sine wave are utilized (e.g., full-wave AC and full-wave rectified AC, or unfiltered full-wave DC).

fuse A protective device, placed in a circuit as a safeguard, that contains a strip of easily melted metal. When the current flow becomes too great, the metal melts, thus breaking the circuit.

gold A very soft, ductile material that is noted for its resistance to corrosive media. It is used primarily as a coating or plating.

ground A conducting connection between an electrical circuit and the earth or other large conducting body to serve as an electrical ground, thus making a complete electrical circuit.

ground, earth The portion of a circuit that is connected to a buried metallic object such as a grounding rod or water pipe.

half-wave Refers to the passing or the use of only one-half of the AC sine wave. The result is half-wave rectified AC, or unfiltered half-wave DC.

hand of door The description of swinging door operation, always viewed from outside the room, building, and so forth. *Left hand* means that the door hinges on the left; *right hand* means that the door hinges on the right.

hard-wired Refers to groups of connections that require the use of wire conductors.

heat sink A method used to transfer a rise in temperature by means of a metal plate or fin-shaped object with good heat transfer efficiency that helps dissipate heat into the surrounding air, into a liquid, or into a larger mass.

heat sink compound   A silicon compound filled with alumina or some other heat-conductive oxide. It is used to fill voids and irregularities in surfaces between two mating objects to permit optimum heat transfer.

Hertz (Hz)   The international unit of frequency equal to one cycle per second; named after the German physicist Heinrich Rudolph Hertz (1857–94).

hi-pot   A test designed to determine the highest potential that can be applied to a conductor without breaking through the insulation.

hookup wire   Insulated wire used for low-current, low-voltage (under 1,000V) applications internally within enclosed electronic equipment.

hot   Connected, alive, energized.

humidity   The amount of moisture in the air, measured in percent of relative humidity.

impedance   The opposition in an electrical circuit to the flow of an alternating current (AC). Impedance consists of ohmic resistance (R), inductive reactance (Xl), and capacitive reactance (Xc).

incandescent lamp   An electric lighting and signaling device that operates on the principle of heating a fine metal wire filament to a white heat by passing an electrical current through it. The filament wire has a positive temperature coefficient that results in high inrush currents, up to ten times the steady state current.

induction   An influence exerted by a charged body or by a magnetic field on neighboring bodies without apparent communication; electrifying, magnetizing, or inducing voltage by exposure to a field.

inductive load   An electric device made of wire, wound or coiled, to create a magnetic field to produce mechanical work when energized. Components such as motors, solenoids, and relay coils are all inductive loads by nature. An inductive load can exhibit an inrush or lock-rotor current of up to five times its normal running or steady state current when energized. When deenergized, the magnetic field collapses and a high-voltage transient is generated, which can cause arcing across contacts or a malfunction of and/or damage to electronic circuits. When transients are present, they should be suppressed. (See *transient*.)

input voltage   The designed power source requirement needed by equipment in order to operate properly.

inrush   The initial surge of current through a load when power is first applied. Lamp loads, inductive motors, solenoids, and capacitive load types all have inrush or surge currents higher than the normal running or steady state currents. Resistive loads, such as heater elements, have no inrush.

insulation   A material that provides high electric resistance, making it suitable for covering components, terminals, and wires to prevent possible future contact of adjacent conductors, resulting in a short circuit.

interlock   A system of multiple doors with controlled interaction. Interlocks are also known as lighttraps, airtraps, mantraps, and sally-ports. (See *safety interlock, security interlock.*)

intermittent duty solenoid   A solenoid designed to be energized for short periods of time. Continuous operation may damage an intermittent duty solenoid.

interval   A period of time from one event to another. An interval timer controls the time for which a load is energized or deenergized.

isolation   No electrical connection between two or more circuits.

jacket   Pertaining to wire and cable, the outer sheath that protects it against the environment and may also provide additional insulation.

jumper   A short length of conductor used to make a connection between terminals, around a break in a circuit, or around an instrument. It is usually a temporary connection.

junction   A point in a circuit where two or more wires are connected.

junction box   A protective enclosure for connecting circuit wires.

keying   The various keying arrangements for pin-tumbler cylinders: *individual key*—the key for an individual cylinder; *keyed alike*—all cylinders may be operated by the same key (not to be confused with *master keyed*); *keyed different*—a different individual key operates each cylinder (or group of cylinders); *master key*—a key to operate a group of cylinders, each of which may be set to a different individual key; *master keyed*—all cylinders in a group can be operated by one master key, although all cylinders may be keyed differently (not to be confused with *keyed alike*).

kilohm   One thousand (10^3) ohms.

labeled   Refers to equipment or materials that have a label, symbol, or other identifying mark of an organization that is approved by the authority having jurisdiction over product evaluation. The label indicates compliance by the manufacturer with appropriate equipment or performance standards.

latch   The locking in of a circuit by means of a holding contact; used in relay logic when a momentary initiation is required.

latchbolt   A device for automatically retaining a door in the closed position upon its closing; a beveled spring-loaded bolt that automatically seats in the strike on contact. Retracted by key cylinder or lever handle.

life   The number of performance hours, days, years, or actual operations for which an item is designed.

light-emitting diode (LED)   A diode, a solid-state device, that gives off virtually heatless colored light when electric current is passed through it. LEDs are very efficient and long-lasting and are often used for digital readouts and annunciators. Common colors include red, green, and amber.

lighttrap or airtrap   A room with two or more doors controlled to prevent more than one door being opened at one time.

line cord   A cord, terminating in a plug at one end, that is used to connect equipment or appliances to a power outlet.

line drop   A voltage loss occurring between any two points in a power or transmission line. Such loss, or drop, is due to the resistance, reactance, or leakage of the line.

line supervision   The electrical supervision of a wire run to detect tampering (a cut or shorted wire). Line supervision usually requires a terminating element at the end of the monitored wire loop. (See *end-of-line resistor*.)

line voltage   The voltage existing in a main cable or circuit, such as at a wall outlet.

listed   Refers to equipment or materials included in a list published by an authorizing organization. The listing states that the equipment or material meets appropriate standards or has been tested for and is suited to a specific application.

load   Any device that consumes electrical power; the amount of power required for operation of a circuit or device.

load rating   A control specification outlining the type of load, the minimum (min.) and the maximum (max.) currents, and the voltage.

local alarm   A visual or audible signaling device located at a monitored door, window, or other opening.

lock   A device for securing a door in the closed position against unauthorized or forced entry. It requires actuation to project or to retract its bolt.

maintained contact switch   A switch designed for applications requiring sustained contact, but with provision for resetting.

make   To close or establish an electrical circuit.

mantrap   See *interlock*.

maximum rating   The absolute maximum condition in which a device is designed to operate. Voltage, frequency, current, temperature, humidity, shock, and other parameters can be specified as maximum.

megohm   One million (10^6) ohms.

mil   One one-thousandth (0.001) of an inch; a unit used in measuring the diameter of wire and the thickness of insulation over a conductor.

milliampere   One one-thousandth (0.001) of an ampere.

millisecond   One one-thousandth (0.001) of a second.

mode of operation   The specified operational condition of a switch, lock, door system, and so forth.

momentary duty lock   An electric lock equipped with a solenoid that is energized only momentarily.

momentary loss of power   A short interruption of power to the total equipment.

momentary switch   A spring-loaded contact that, when pressed, closes two contacts. When pressure is removed, the contacts open.

monitoring loop   A continuous loop of wire starting at the control panel and running through switches in a system to indicate a breach of security through an open switch or a cut wire.

mother board   A master printed circuit board used to interface the activities of individual printed circuit boards and the devices being controlled or monitored. The mother board is usually located at the back of a control panel assembly; individual printed circuit boards plug into it.

multiconductor cable   A cable consisting of two or more conductors, either cabled or laid in a flat parallel construction, with or without a common overall covering.

multiplex   Refers to a system of transmitting several messages simultaneously on the same circuit or channel. Multiplex equipment greatly reduces the number of wire cables needed in a system.

National Electrical Code (NEC)   A consensus standard published by the National Fire Protection Association (NFPA); commonly called "code."

National Electrical Manufacturers Association (NEMA) An organization known for its standardization of wire and cable specifications.

noise Unwanted and/or unintelligible signals picked up on a cable circuit.

normally closed (NC) The condition or position of a contact prior to initiation or energization—in this case, a closed condition.

normally open (NO) The condition or position of a contact prior to initiation or energization—in this case, an open condition.

occupancy indicator A visual indication to service personnel that a room is occupied; consists of a small pin in the outside cylinder that is extended by pressing the inside button.

octal plug An eight-pin male connector with a locating key for proper orientation.

ohm A unit of measurement for resistance (R) and impedance (Z).

Ohm's law One of the most widely used principles of electricity. It expresses the relationship between voltage (E), current (I) and resistance (R) according to the following equations: $E = IR$; $I = E/R$; $R = E/I$.

operating temperature A temperature range over which a device will perform within its specified design tolerances; may be stated in degrees Fahrenheit (°F) or degrees centigrade (°C).

operating voltage The voltage by which a system operates; a nominal voltage with a specified tolerance applied; the design voltage range necessary to remain within the operating tolerances. For example, for a system specified 120 volts $+/-$ 10 percent of nominal, 120 volts is the nominal voltage and the design voltage range is 108 to 132 volts AC.

output voltage The designed power source produced by a power supply to operate equipment.

panic-proof locks Locks that provide immediate exit from the inside at all times.

parallel A method of connecting an electric circuit whereby each element is connected across the other. The addition of all currents through each element equals the total current of the circuit.

passbox A wall opening between rooms through which material is transferred.

polarity The positive or negative orientation of a signal or power source.

potentiometer (pot) Variable resistor.

primary   The transformer winding that receives the energy from a supply circuit.

printed circuit board   A means of making electrical interconnections without using insulated wires. Printed circuit boards provide a supporting and insulating medium for components and conductors in a form that is readily adaptable to machine assembly.

rack-mounted   Refers to a method of housing many control and security panels. Nineteen-inch rack mounting is a standard for the electrical equipment trades. Rack mounting allows equipment of several different manufacturers, different types of communications, fire/smoke alarm, and security equipment to be used in the same area without taking up a large amount of space. It also achieves a more uniform and organized appearance.

rated voltage   The maximum voltage at which an electric component can operate for extended periods without undue degradation or safety hazard.

reactance   Opposition offered to the flow of alternating current by inductance or capacitance of a component or circuit.

rectifier   A solid state electrical device that will allow current to flow in one direction only. It is designed to convert alternating current to direct current.

recycle time   The time needed to reset and reinitiate the timing function and remain within the specified timing tolerances. Recycle time is generally specified "during timing" or "after timing."

regulated power supply   A power supply that provides a constant output regardless of input voltage variations.

relay   An electrically controlled device that opens and closes electrical contacts to effect the operation of other devices in the same or another electrical circuit.

remote alarm   A visual or audible signaling device used to signal violations at locations removed from the central control station or monitored openings. For example, a remote alarm may be placed on a roof, in a stair tower, or at guard stations outside a building.

remote reset   A switch located at a monitored opening. If a violation occurs, the alarm at the main control console cannot be turned off until the door is secured and the remote reset is activated. Its purpose is to ensure the inspection of an opening that has been violated or left open.

reset time The time required to return the output to its original condition.

resistance The opposition to the flow of an electric current (measured in ohms); the reciprocal of conductance.

resistor A circuit element whose chief purpose is to oppose the flow of current.

resolution The degree of setability.

reverse polarity protected Applies to DC controls where, if the polarity of the input were reversed, there would be no damage.

rigid conduit A metal piping for housing the insulated wires of an electric circuit.

riser diagram A document which explains wire type, size, and the number of conductors to be run from a control panel to each control or monitor location.

root-mean-square (rms) A term applied to alternating voltage and current that means the effective value; that is, it produces the same heating effect as a direct current or voltage of the same magnitude. It is also a means of expressing AC voltage in terms of DC (usually approximately 80 percent of the AC peak voltage).

safety interlock A multidoor system in which all doors are normally closed and unlocked; opening any door locks all other doors.

sallyport See *interlock*.

secondary The transformer winding that receives energy by electromagnetic induction from the primary.

security interlock A multidoor system in which all doors are normally closed and locked; releasing one door disables the releases for all other doors until the first door is closed and relocked.

semiconductor A material that has a resistance between that of insulators and conductors.

series circuit An electrical circuit in which all the receptive devices are arranged in succession, as distinguished from a parallel circuit. The same current flows through each part of the circuit in sequence.

shield In cables, a metallic layer placed around a conductor or group of conductors to prevent electrostatic interference between the enclosed wires and external fields.

short An improper connection between "hot" current-carrying wire and neutral or ground.

silver   A metal, similar to gold in corrosion resistance, that costs less than other precious metals. It is very soft when fully annealed but work-hardens during fabrication. It provides very good conductivity and solderability. It is widely used as a plating or coating.

single pole, double throw (SPDT)   A term used to describe a switch or relay contact form (1 form C) that has a normally open and a normally closed contact with a common connection.

single pole, single throw (SPST)   A switch with only one moving and one stationary contact, available either normally open (NO) or normally closed (NC).

solenoid   An electromechanical device that operates the lockbolt. When electricity is applied, a mechanical motion is obtained that moves the bolt.

soldering   A method of making an electrical connection. The two components to be connected are physically placed together and heated. Solder, a conductive metallic alloy with a low melting point, is then placed on the heated components. It melts and flows around the components to make a permanent connection.

spike   A momentary increase in electrical current. Spikes can damage electronic equipment.

splice   A connection of two or more conductors or cables to provide good mechanical strength as well as good conductivity.

springlatch   A plain latch with a beveled latchbolt that is activated by springs.

standard duty locking unit   An electric lock equipped with a solenoid that is energized for short periods of time, not continuously.

steady state   A term used to specify the current through a load or electric circuit after the inrush current is complete; a stable run condition.

storage temperature   The maximum temperature that any one material in a system can withstand without sustaining damage; a nonworking condition.

stranded conductor   A conductor composed of several single solid wires twisted together.

strike   A plate mortised into or mounted on the door jamb to accept and restrain a bolt when the door is closed. In some metal installations of a deadlock, the strike may simply be an opening cut into the jamb. (Synonym: *keeper*.)

supervised circuit   A circuit that will indicate alarm and trouble conditions.

switches   Devices that make or break connections in an electrical or electronic circuit. In computing systems, they are also used to make selections (the toggle switch, for example, completes a conditional jump). Switches are usually manually operated but can also work by mechanical, thermal, electromechanical, barometric, hydraulic, or gravitational means.

switch, momentary   A switch that, when activated, automatically returns to its original position afterwards.

switch, maintained   A switch that, when activated, maintains its activated position until it is unactivated.

switch, normally open   A switch that, when not energized, is open and does not permit current to flow.

switch, normally closed   A switch that, when not energized, is closed to form a path for current.

tap   A special lead brought out from an intermediate point of a coil or winding.

telephone wire   A very general term referring to many different types of communication wire. It refers to a class of wires and cables, rather than a specific type.

terminal block   A device that provides a place for safe and convenient interconnection of current-carrying conductors.

terminals   Metal wire termination devices designed to handle one or more conductors and to be attached to a board, bus, or block with mechanical fasteners or clipped on. Common types are ring tongue, spade, flag, hook, blade, quick-connect, offset, flanged. Special types include taper pin, taper tab, and others, either insulated or noninsulated.

terminating element   An electric device connected at the end of a pair of electrical conductors that provides the means of supervising those conductors. (See *line supervision*.)

time delay   An electronically controlled delay period designed into a component that will either send a prolonged signal or delay transmitting a signal.

time-delay relay   A relay for automatically locking or unlocking a locking unit after a short, fixed time interval.

tinned copper   Copper with a tin coating added to aid in soldering and to inhibit corrosion.

tolerance   Normally stated as a percentage, the maximum allowable deviation of electrical, environmental, or dimensional parameters.

transformer   An electric device that changes voltage in direct proportion to currents and in inverse proportion to the ratio of the number of turns of its primary and secondary windings. The input side of a transformer is called the primary side; the output or low-voltage side is called the transformer secondary.

transient   Any increase or decrease in the excursion of voltage, current, power, heat, and so forth, above or below a nominal value that is not normal to the source. (See *transient voltage*.)

transient voltage   Refers to several parameters of a transient: (1) the peak or maximum voltage reached, (2) the rate of rise of the transient (dv/dt), and (3) the duration of the transient. Transient voltages are generated when inductive loads such as solenoids, contactors, motors, relays, and so forth, are deenergized. Although some devices have excellent protection against these sometimes damaging excursions, when a transient is known to be present, it should be suppressed at the source. Diodes and metal oxide varistors (MOVs) are commonly used as suppressors.

trickle charge   A low-powered electrical energy source provided to keep standby batteries fully charged.

twisted pair   A cable composed of two small insulated conductors, twisted together without a common covering. The two conductors of a twisted pair are usually substantially insulated, so the combination is a special case of a cord.

volt (V)   A unit of electromotive force. It is the difference of potential required to make a current of one ampere flow through a resistance of one ohm.

voltage   The term most often used (in place of *electromotive force, potential, potential difference,* or *voltage drop*) to designate electrical pressure that exists between two points and is capable of producing a flow of current when a closed circuit is connected between the two points.

voltage drop   Voltage loss experienced by electrical circuits due to two principal factors: (1) wire size and (2) length of wire runs.

volt/amp (VA) rating   The product of rated input voltage multiplied by the rated current. This establishes the "apparent energy" available to accomplish work.

watt   The common unit of electrical power. One watt is dissipated by a resistance of one ohm through which one ampere flows.

wire   A slender rod or filament of drawn metal.

wire nut   A connector used to make and insulate an electrical connection. Wire ends are stripped and placed into a caplike connector (wire nut), and the wire-nut is then twisted to secure the wire ends together. The cap design serves to insulate the connection.

zone   A specific area of protection; a portion of a large protected area.

Bibliography

For further study in a particular area, the following books provide excellent information.

Electric Locks

Electric Strike Manual, by Bill G. Nail, as told to Fred T. Potter. City of Industry, CA: Adams Rite Manufacturing Co., 1977.

Electrical Wiring and Codes

The National Electrical Code® Handbook, edited by Peter J. Schram. Quincy, MA: National Fire Protection Association, 1983.
Practical Electrical Wiring, by Herbert P. Richter and W. Creighton Schwan. New York: McGraw-Hill, 1984.

Mechanical Locks

All About Locks and Locksmithing, by Max Alth. New York: Hawthorn Books, 1972.
Collectible Locks, by Richard Holiner. Paducah, KY: Collector Books, 1979.
Locks and Keys, by T. M. Hennesey. Des Plaines, IL: Nickerson and Collins, 1976.
Unlocking Adventure, by Charles Courtney and Thomas M. Johnson. New York: McGraw-Hill, 1942.

Index